Learn Shapes
with Camron & Chloe

Denver International SchoolHouse

Learn Shapes with Camron & Chloe

Denver International SchoolHouse

© 2020 Denver International SchoolHouse

All rights reserved. No part of this publication may be reproduced, stored in a retrieval system or transmited in any form or by any means, electronic, mechanical, photocopying, recording or otherwise without the prior permision of the publisher or in accordance with the provisions of the Copyright, Designs and Patents Act 1988 or under the terms of any licence permitting limited copying issued by the Copyright Licensing Angency.

ISBN : 978-1-7358013-5-3

Name:_____

Circle

Trace the **circles**.

Trace the word.

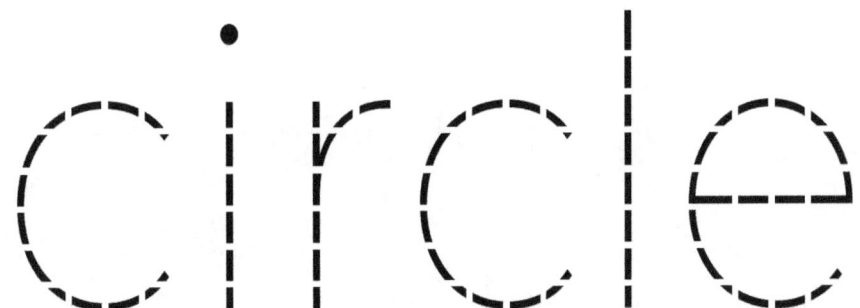

Denver International SchoolHouse

Name:_____

Circle

Trace the *circles*.

Denver International SchoolHouse

Name:_____

Circle

Trace each *circle* and color the picture.

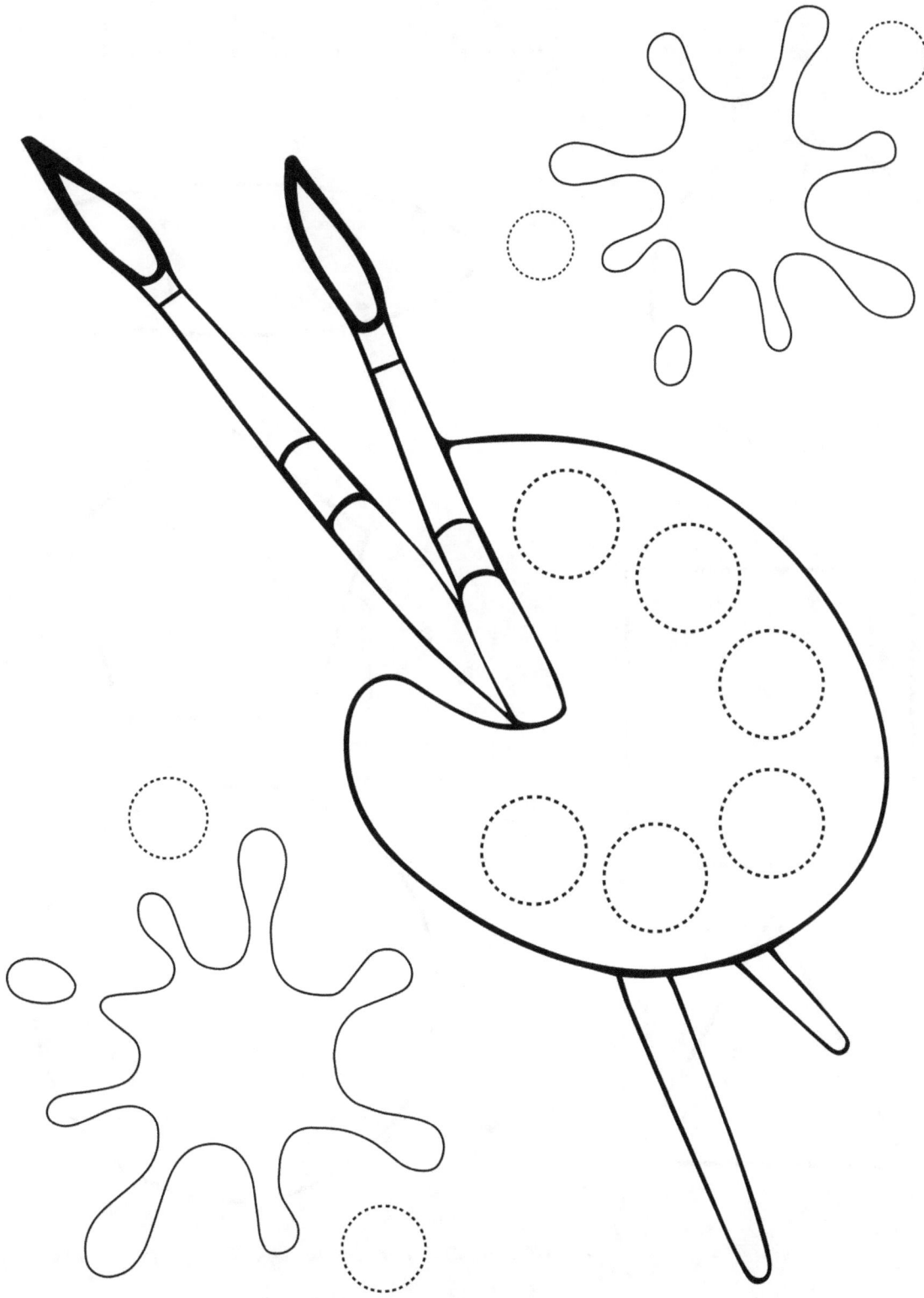

Name:_____

Circle

Color the *circle*.

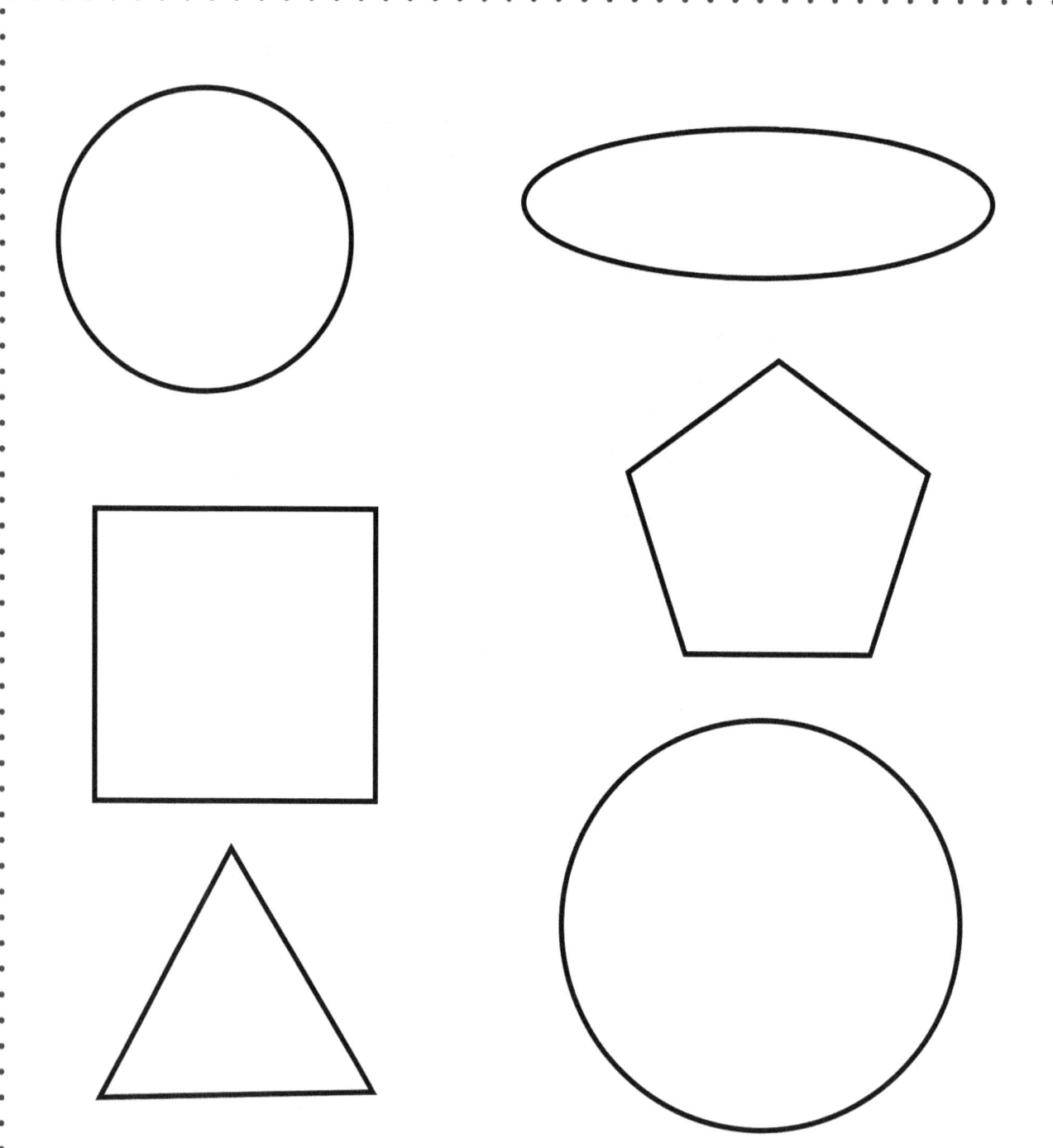

Name:_____

Trace, color and write

Trace and color each **circle** with the correct crayon.

Read the word. Trace the word. Then, write the word on your own.

| circle | circle |

Name:_____

Circle

*Practice drawing **circles**.*

*Practice writing **circle** on your own.*

Name:_____

Square

Trace the **squares**.

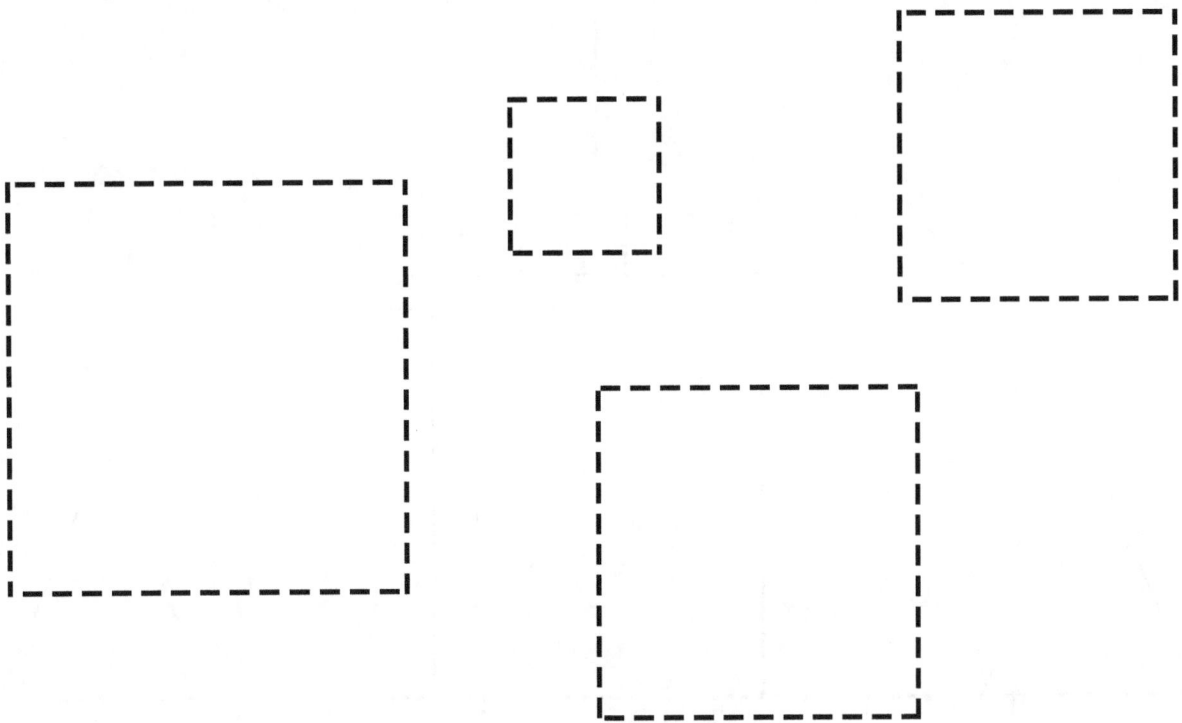

Trace the word.

square

Name:_____

Square

Trace the **squares**.

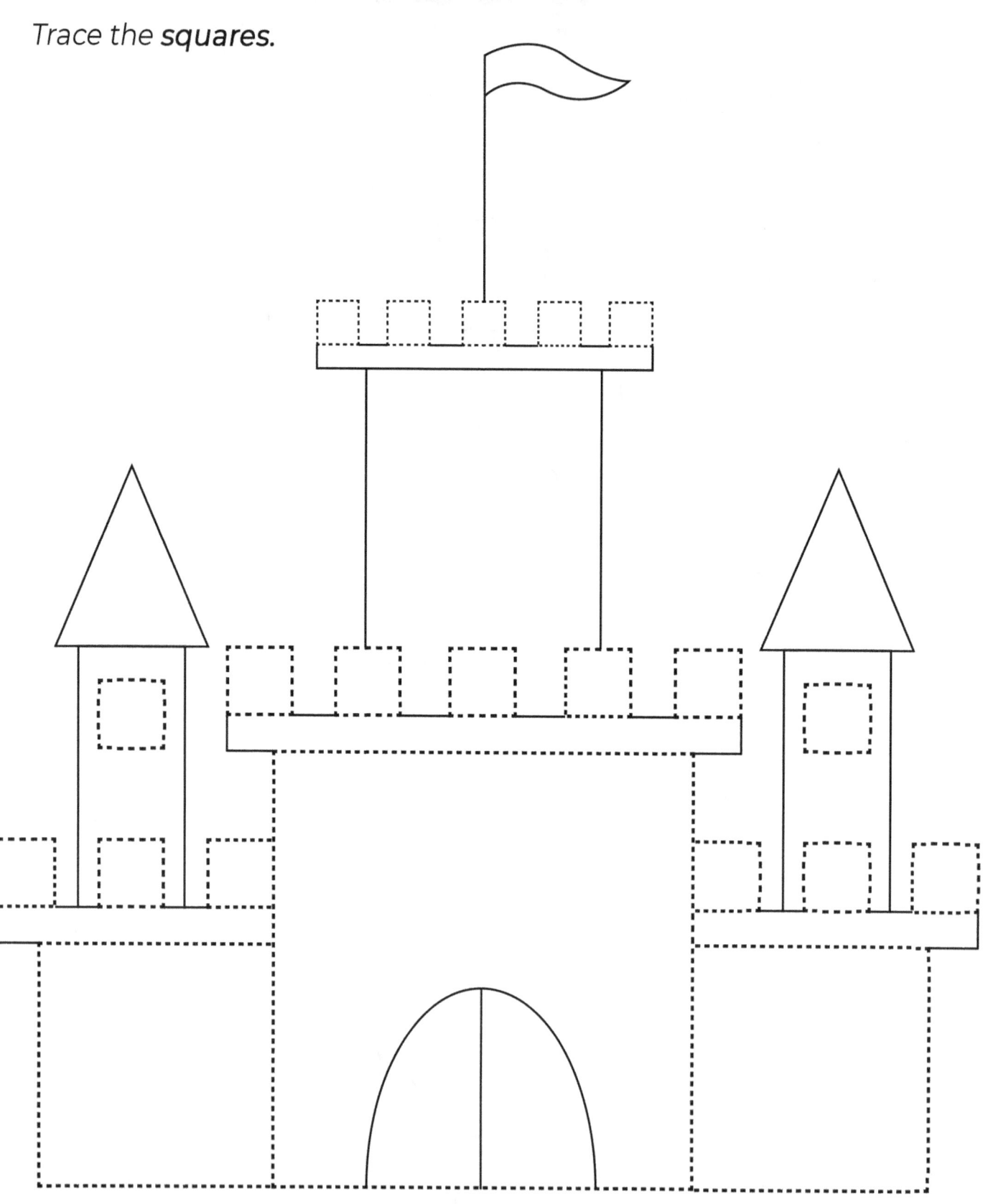

Name:_____

Square

Trace each *square* and color the picture.

Denver International SchoolHouse

Name:_____

Square

Color the *squares*.

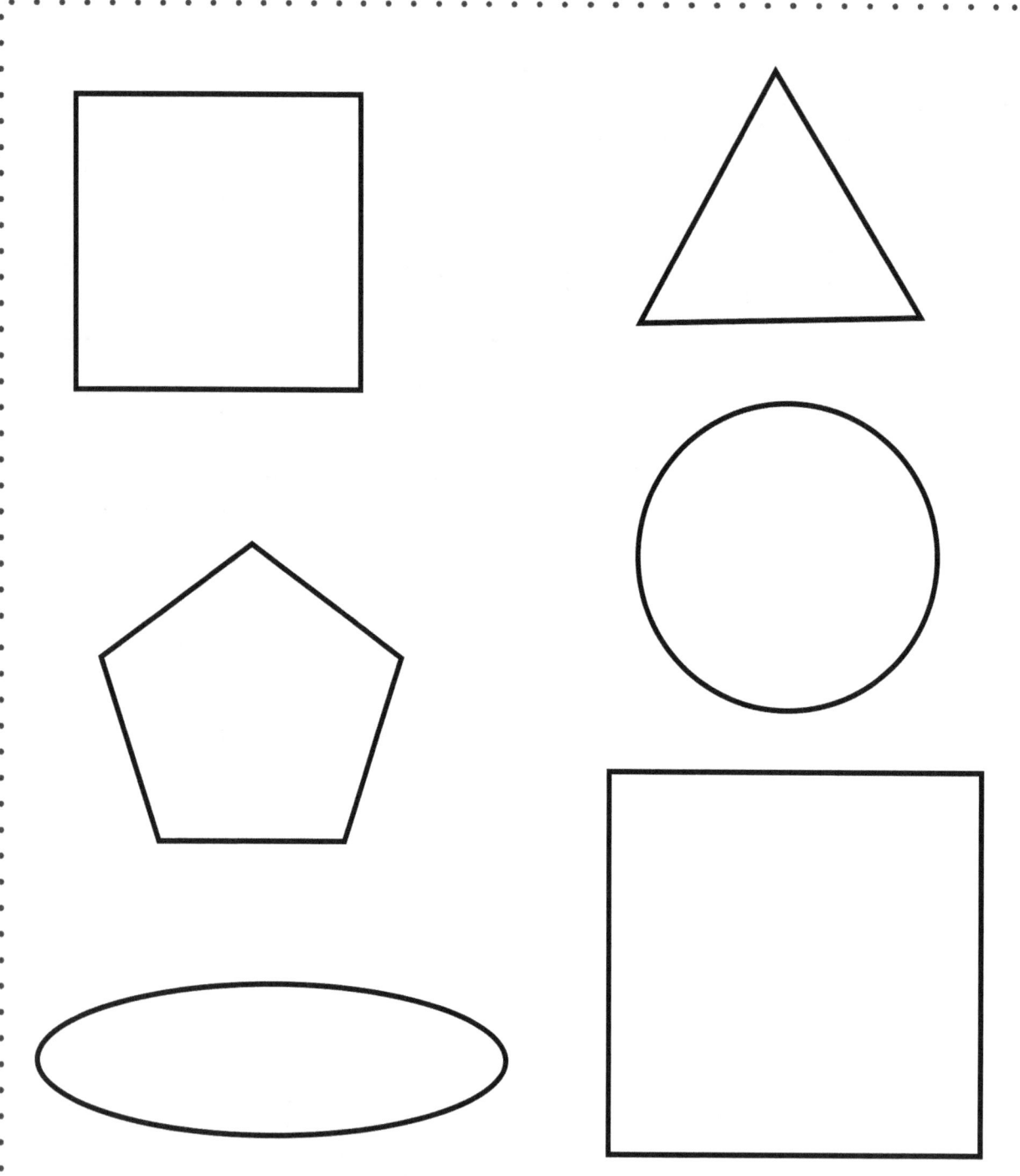

Name:_____

Trace, color and write

Trace and color each *square* with the correct crayon.

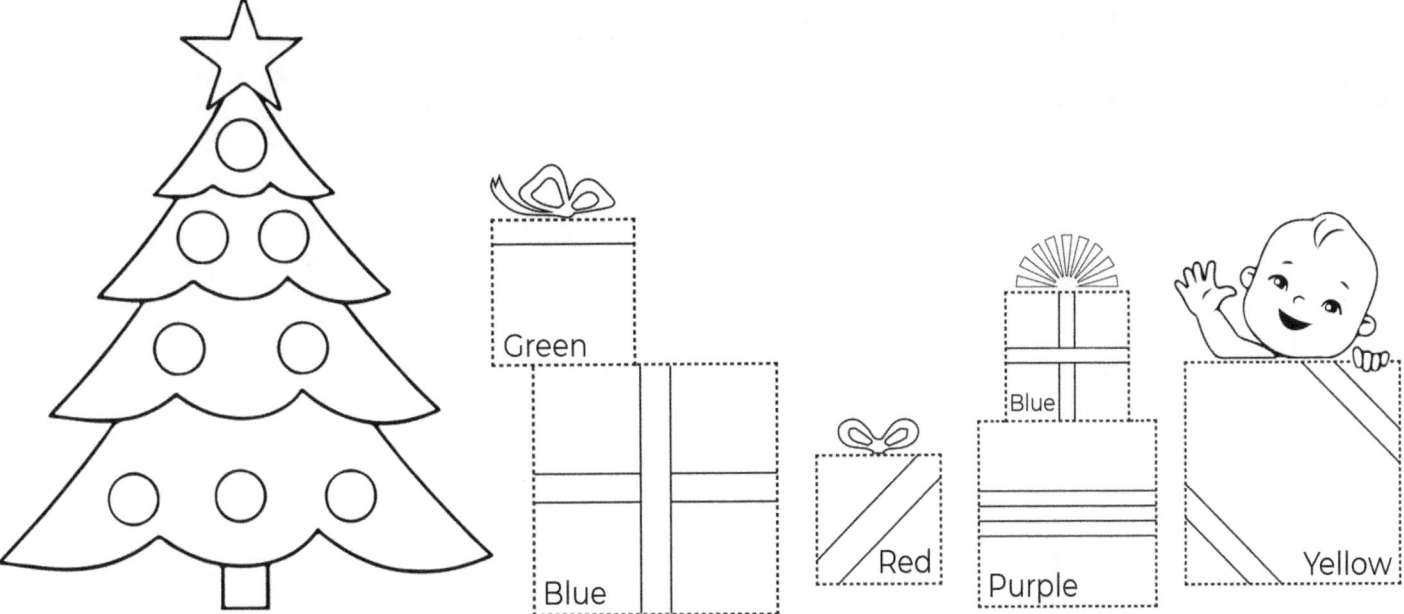

Read the word. Trace the word. Then, write the word on your own.

| square | square |

11   Denver International SchoolHouse

Name:_____

Square

Practice drawing **squares**.

Practice writing **square** on your own.

Denver International SchoolHouse

Name:_____

Cube

Trace the **cubes**.

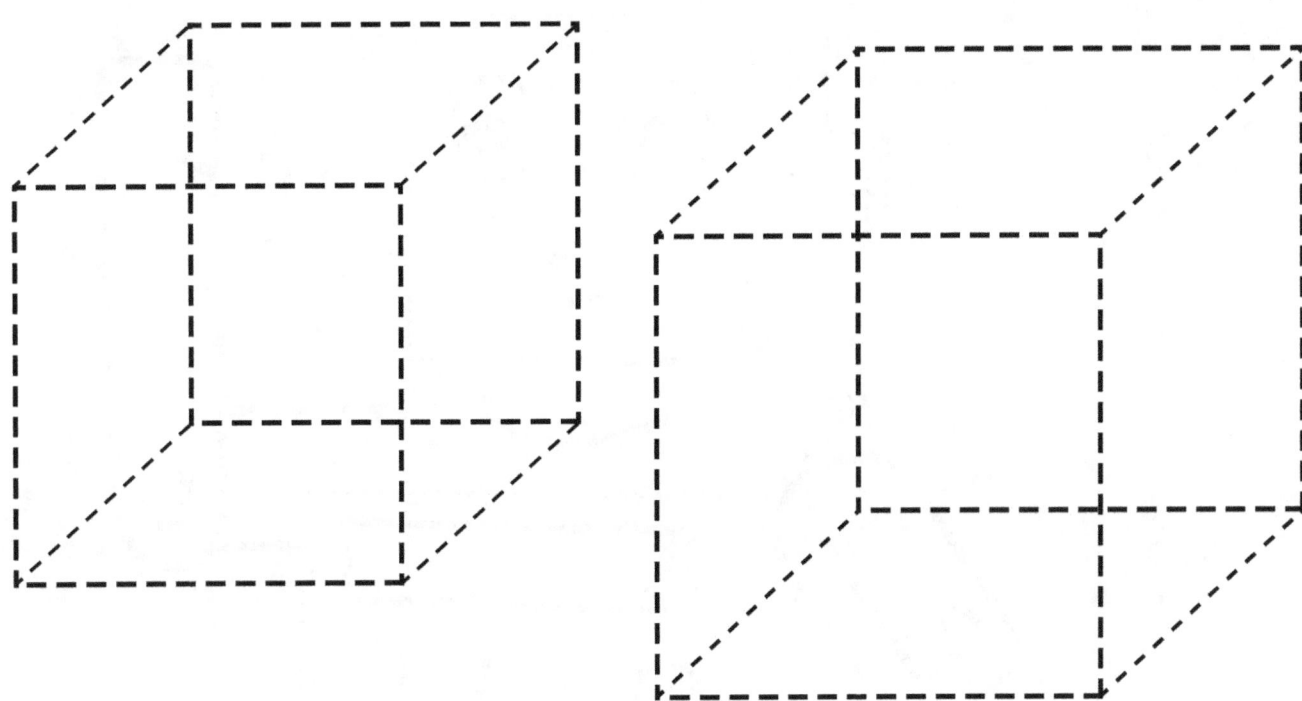

Trace the word.

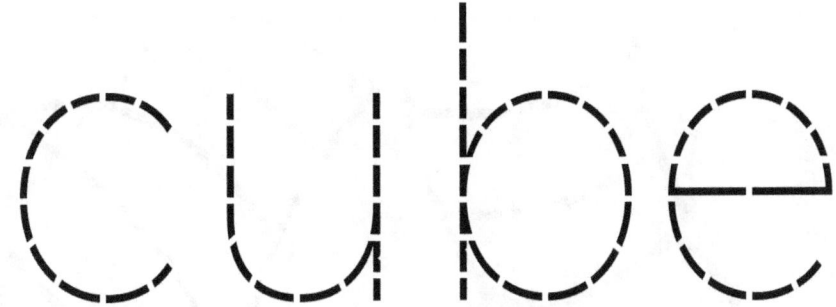

Name:_____

Cube

Trace the **cubes.**

Denver International SchoolHouse

Name:_____

Cube

Trace each **cube** and color the picture.

15   Denver International SchoolHouse

Cube

Name:_____

Color the **cubes**.

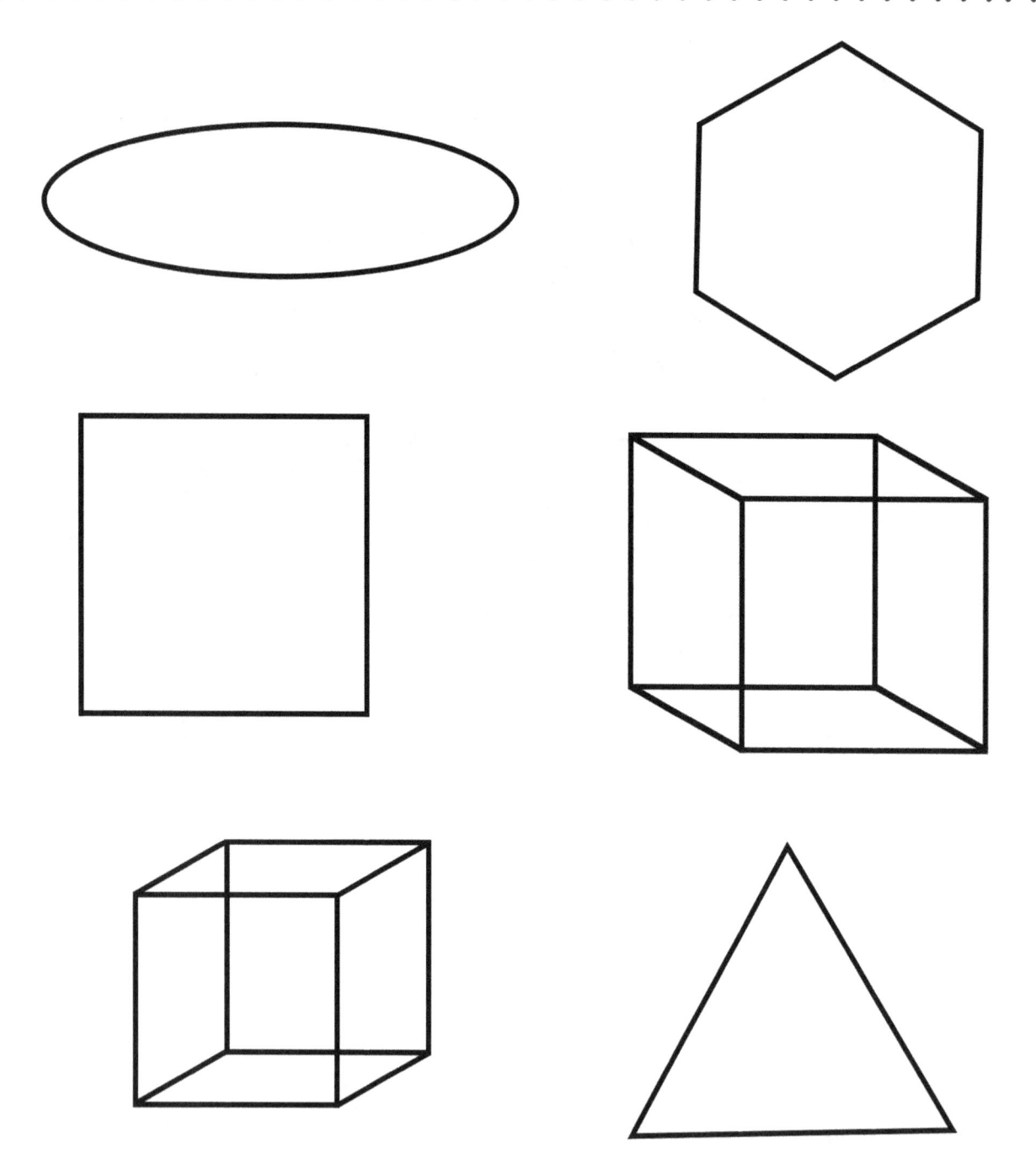

Name:_____

Trace, color and write

Trace and color each **cube** with the correct crayon.

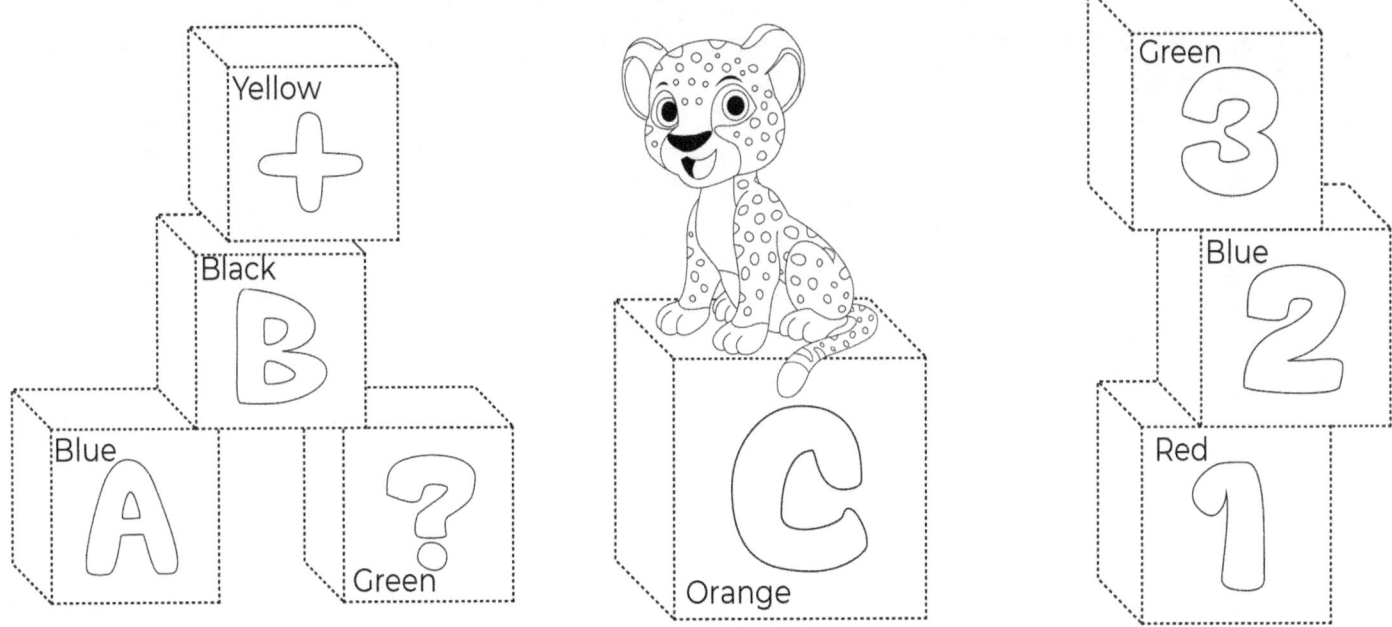

Read the word. Trace the word. Then, write the word on your own.

| cube | cube |

_____
- -
_____

Name:_____

Cube

Practice drawing **cubes**.

Practice writing **cube** on your own.

Name:_____

Triangle

Trace the **Triangle**.

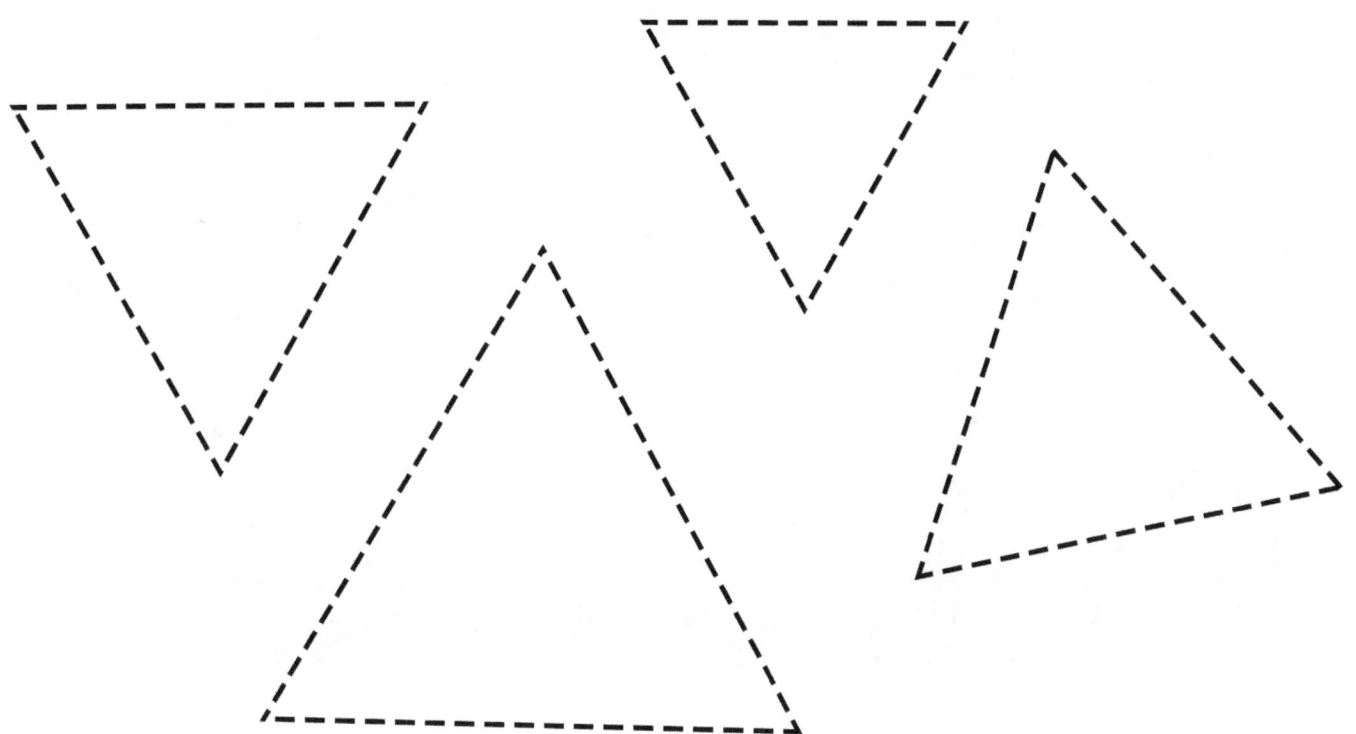

Trace the word.

Denver International SchoolHouse

Triangle

Name:_____

Trace the *triangle*.

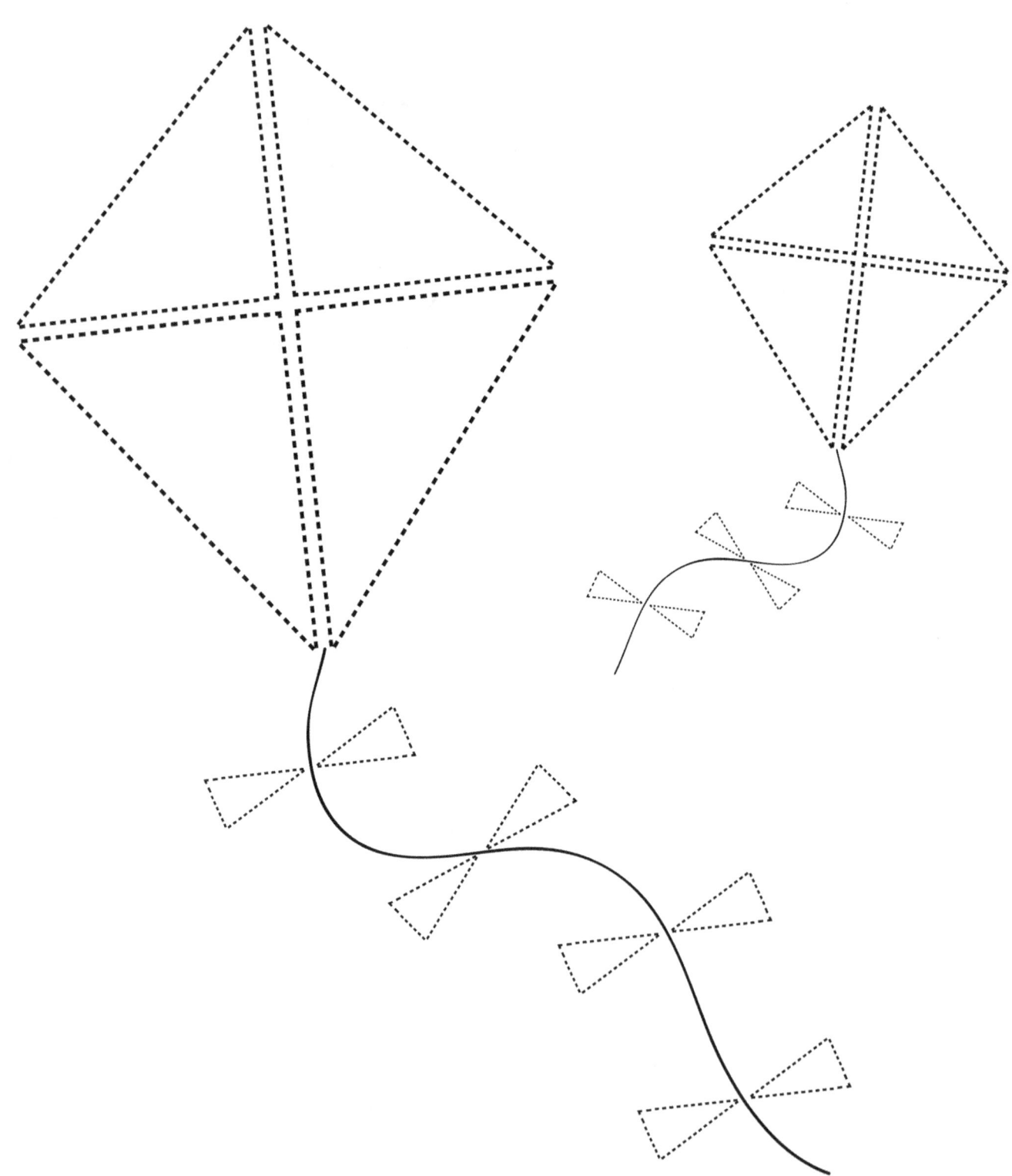

Name:_____

Triangle

Trace each **triangle** and color the picture.

21　　　　　　　　　　Denver International SchoolHouse

Triangle

Name:_____

Color the **triangle**.

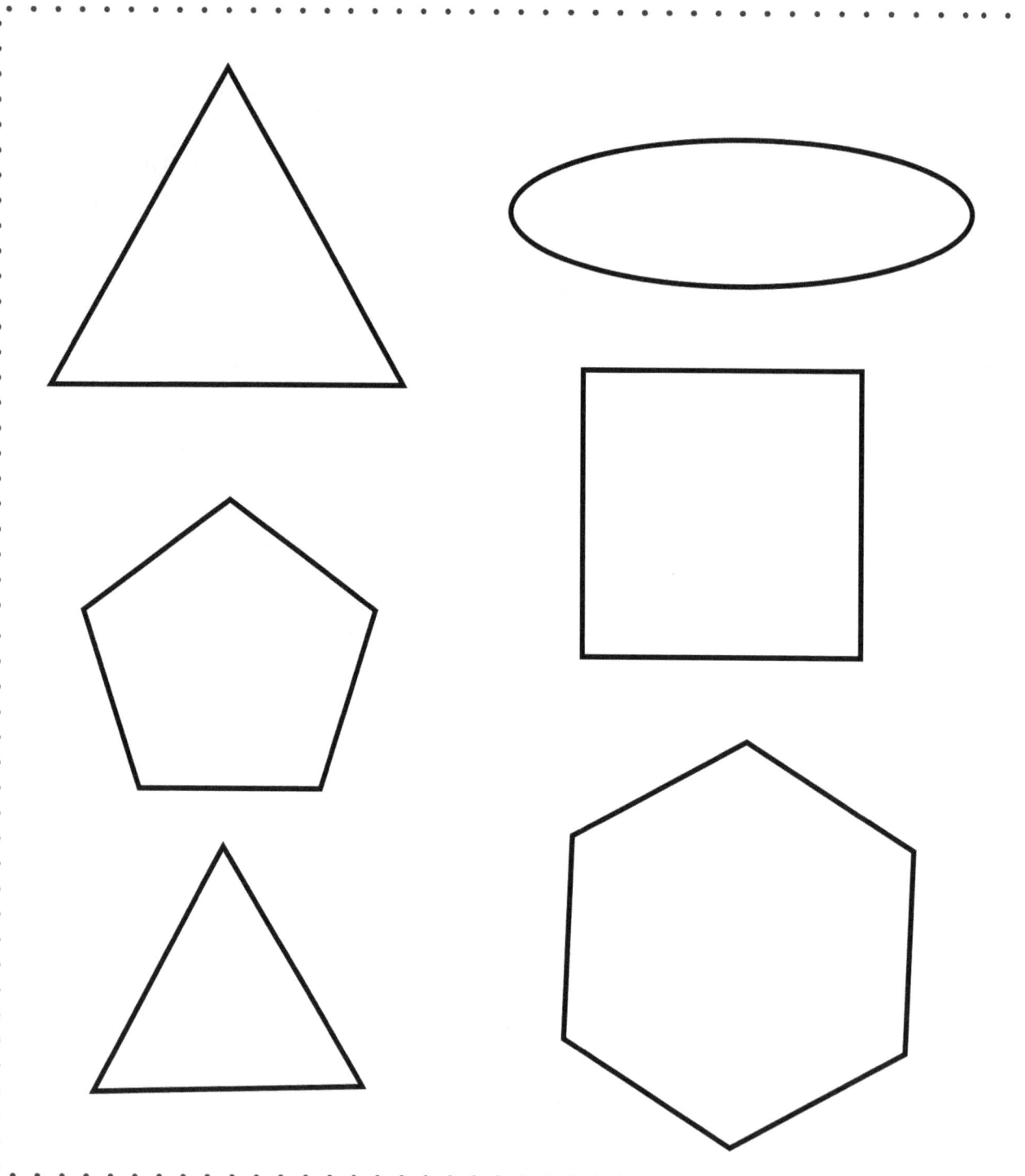

Name:_____

Trace, color and write

Trace and color each **triangle** with the correct crayon.

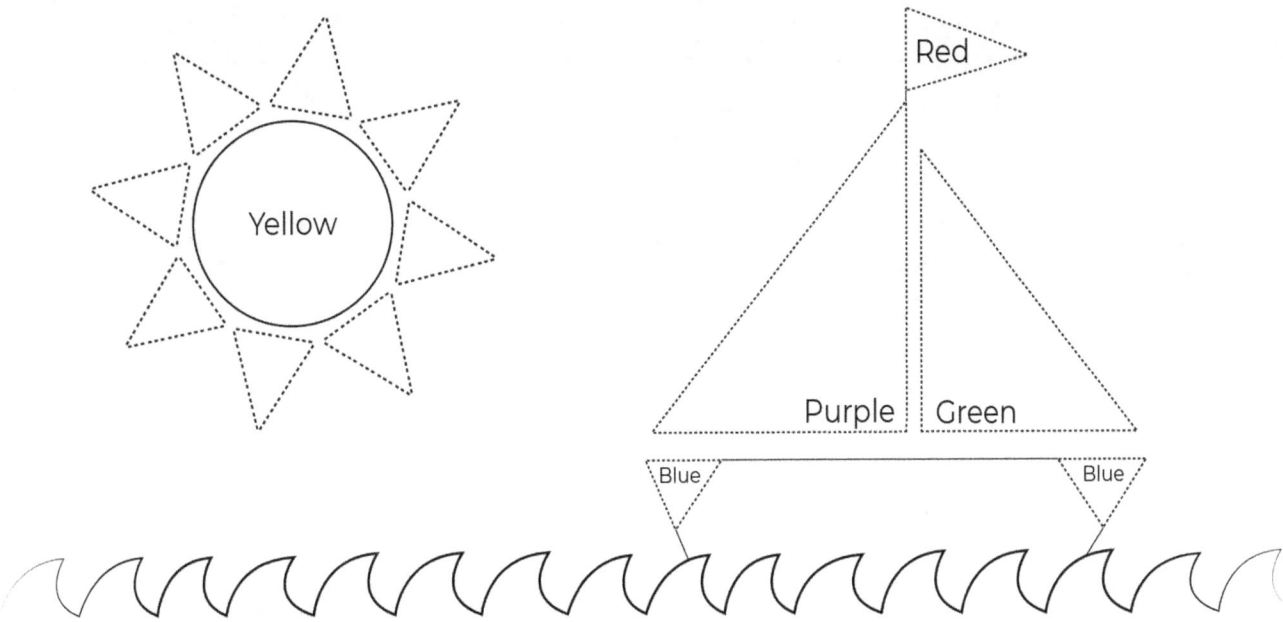

Read the word. Trace the word. Then, write the word on your own.

| triangle | triangle |

23 Denver International SchoolHouse

Name:_____

Triangle

*Practice drawing **triangles**.*

*Practice writing **triangle** on your own.*

Name:_____

Trapezoid

Trace the **trapezoids**.

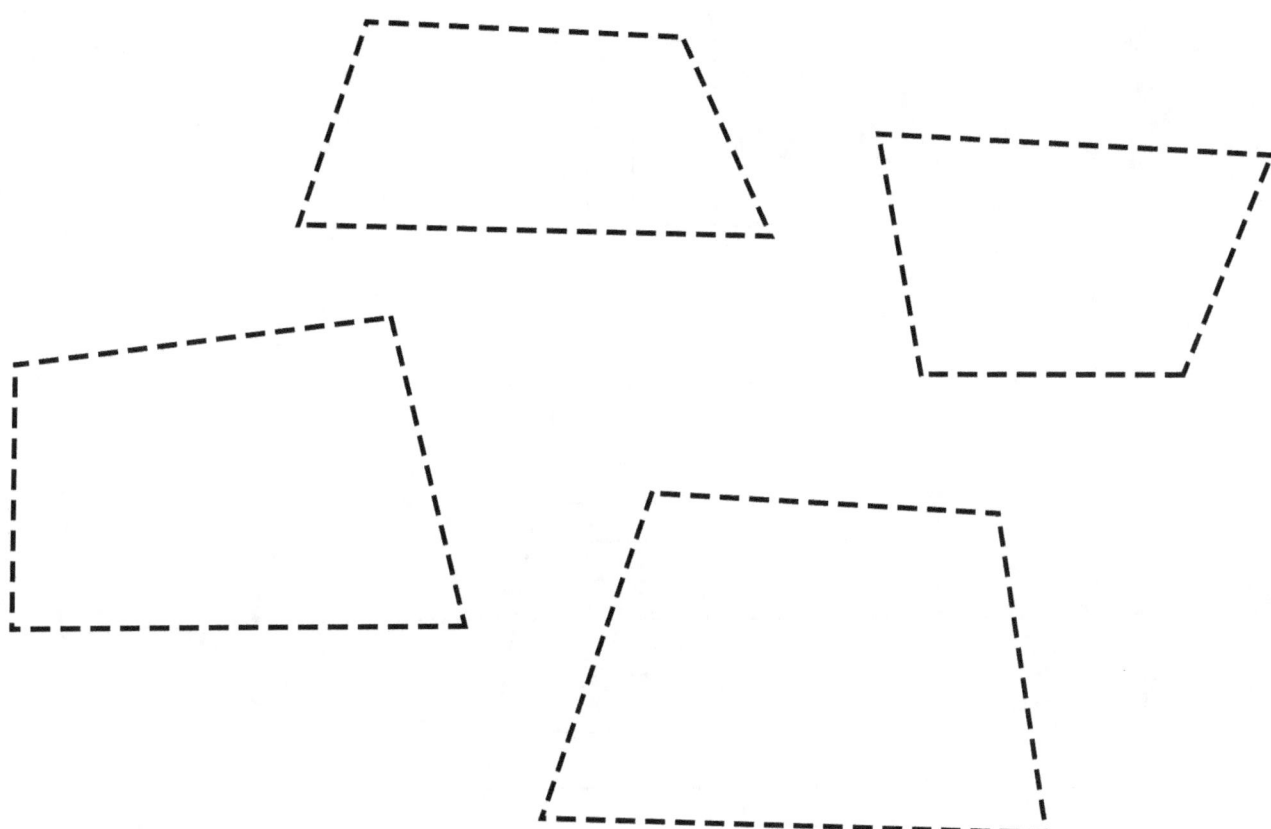

Trace the word.

trapezoid

Name:_____

Trapezoid

Trace the *trapezoids*.

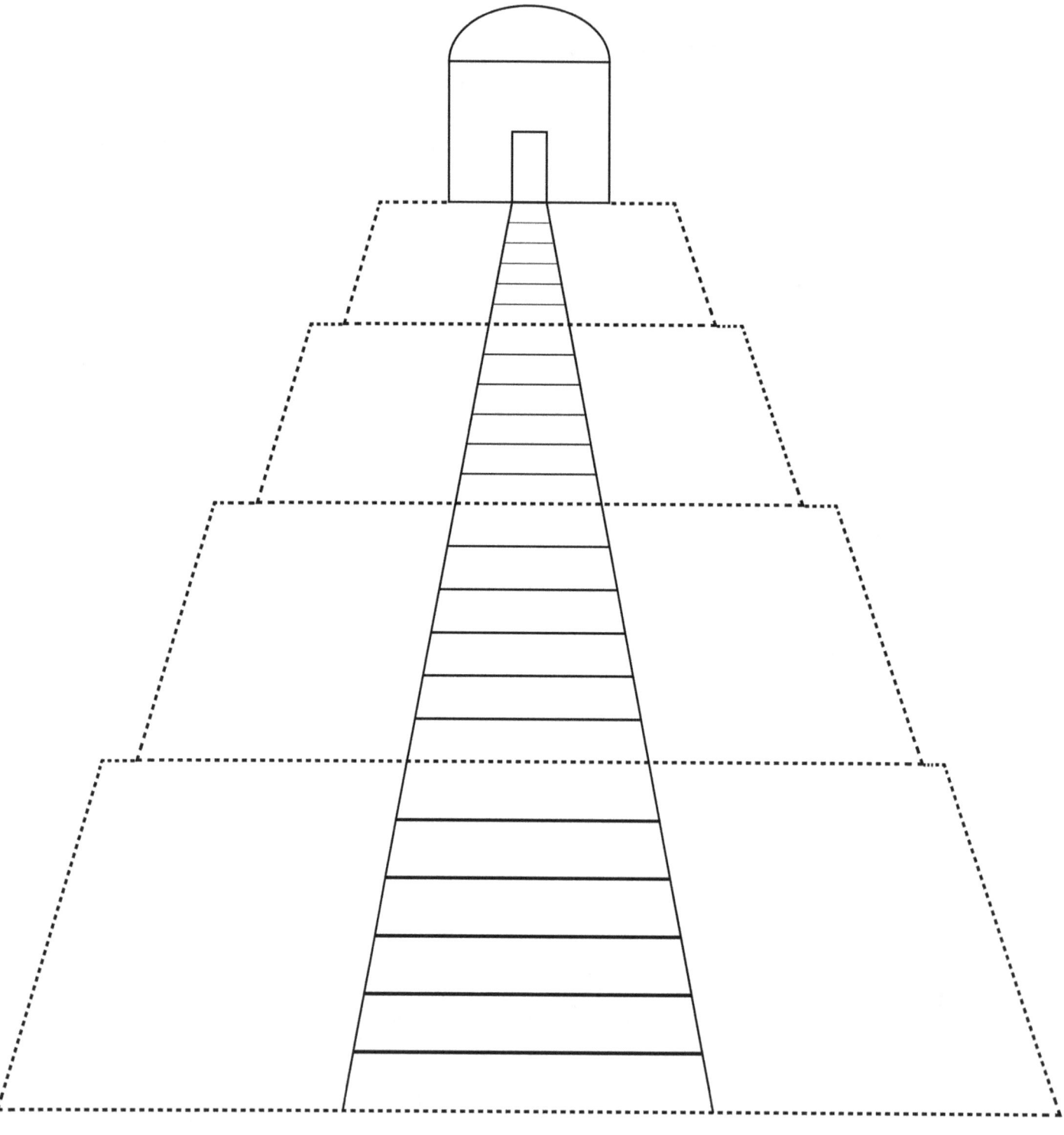

Denver International SchoolHouse 26

Name:_____

Trapezoid

Trace each **trapeziod** and color the picture.

27   Denver International SchoolHouse

Name:_____

Trapezoid

*Color the **trapezoids**.*

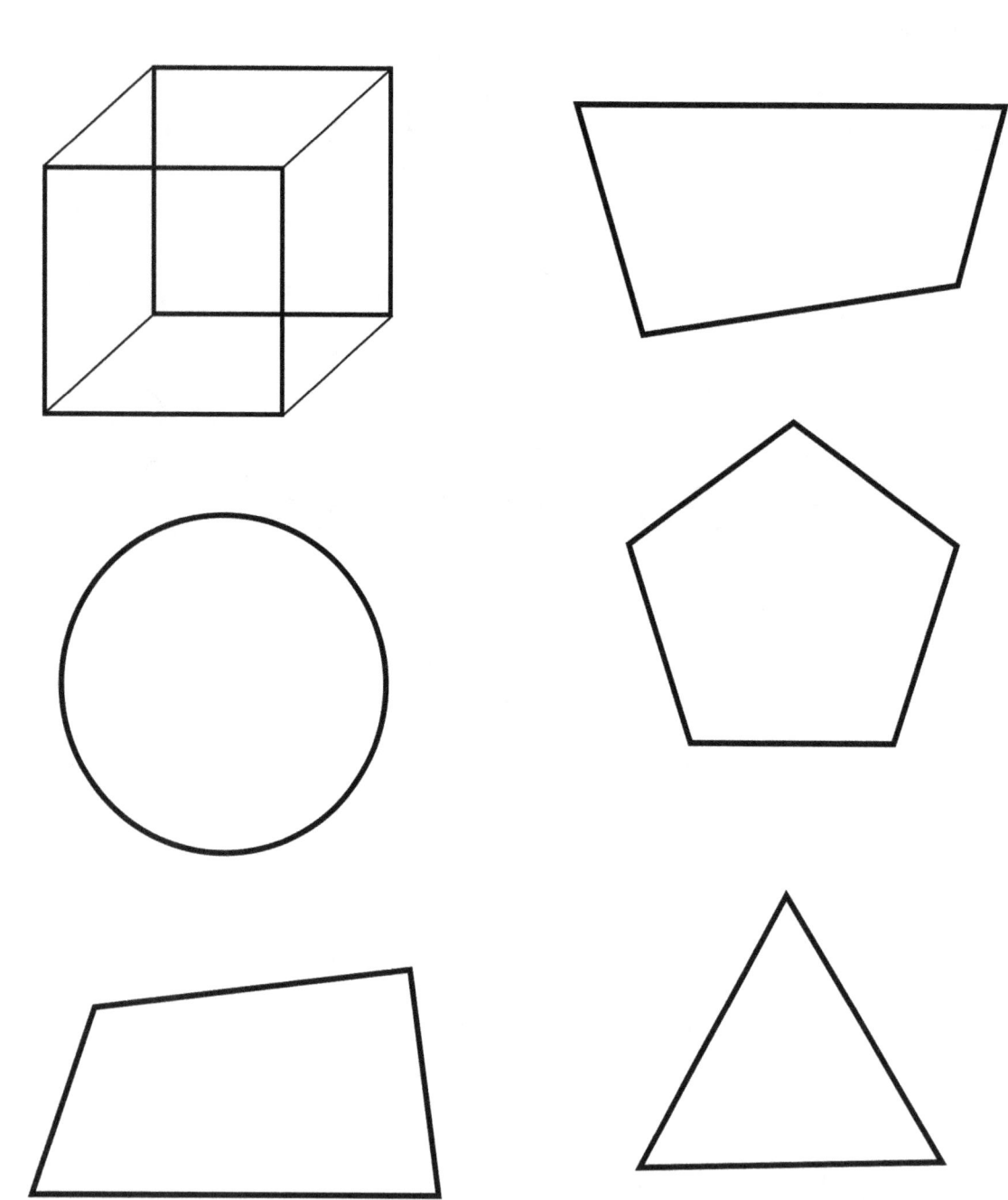

Name:_____

Trace, color and write

Trace and color each **trapezoid** with the correct crayon.

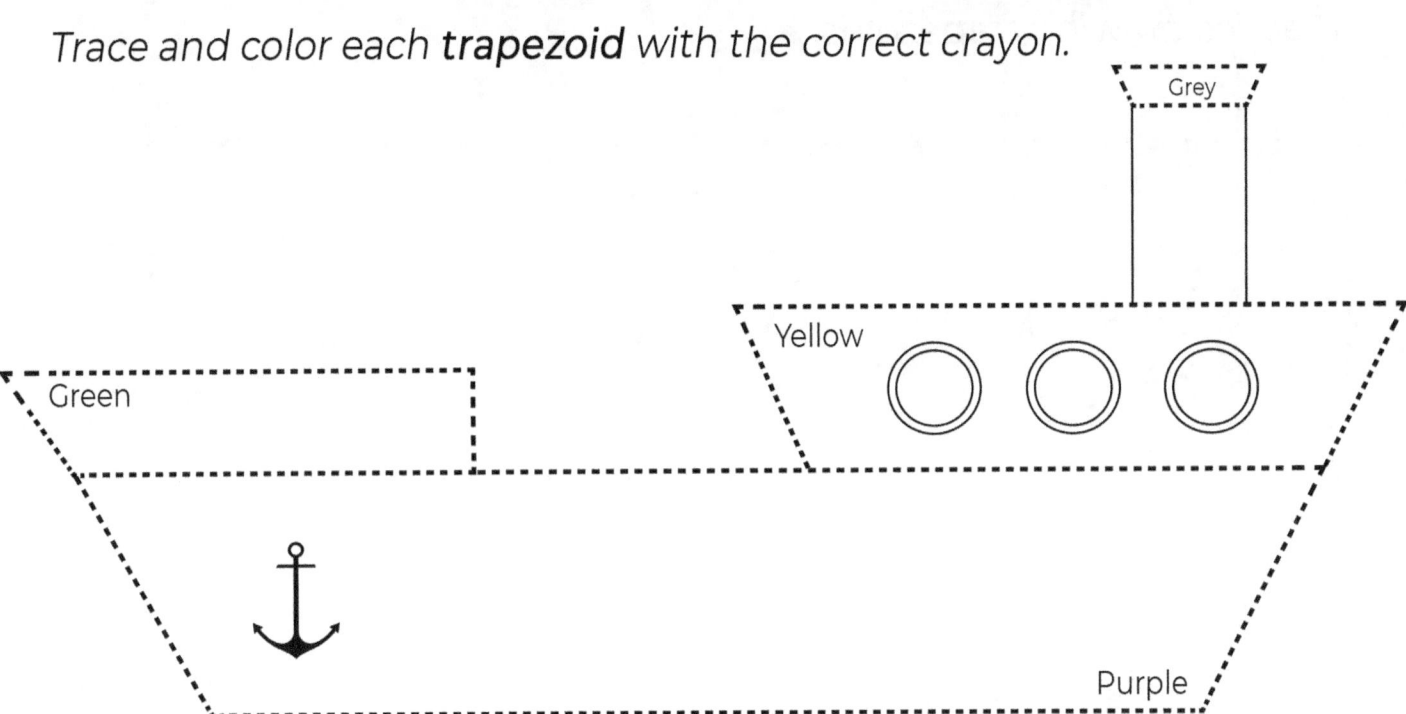

Read the word. Trace the word. Then, write the word on your own.

| trapezoid | trapezoid |

Name:_____

Trapezoid

*Practice drawing **trapezoids**.*

*Practice writing **trapezoid** on your own.*

Name:_____

Rectangle

Trace the **rectangles**.

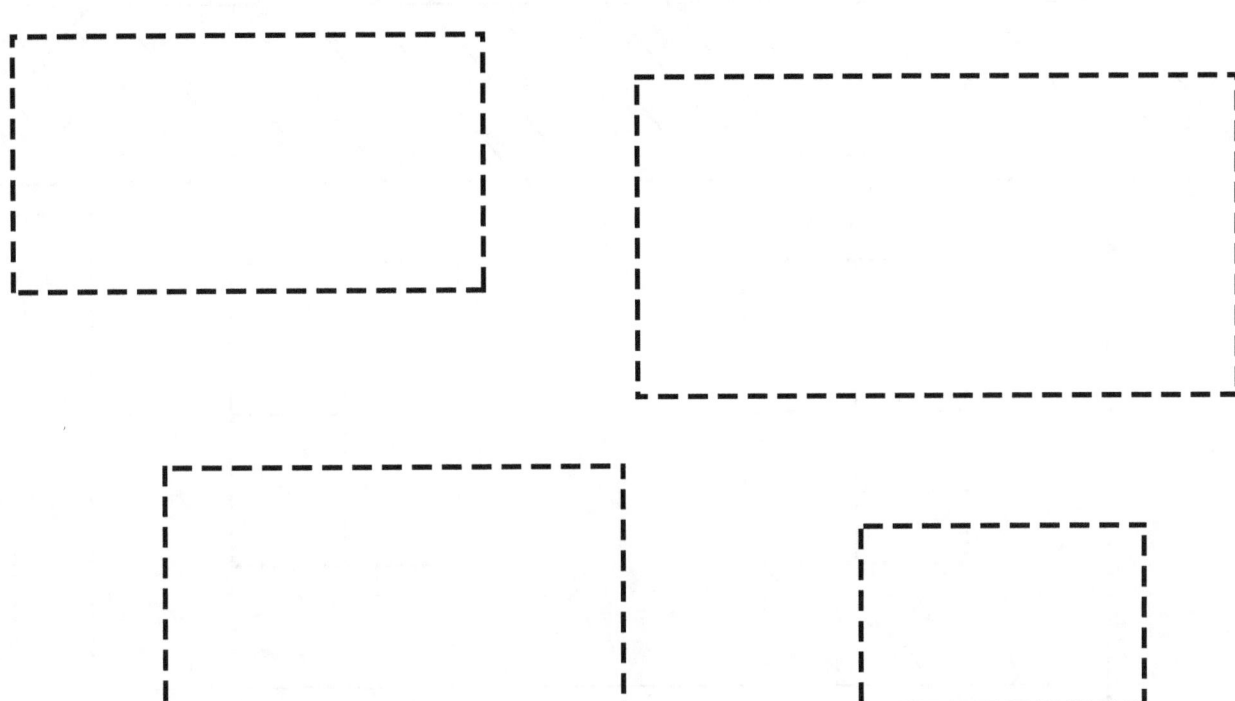

Trace the word.

rectangle

Name:_____

Rectangle

Trace the **rectangles**.

Denver International SchoolHouse

Name:_____

Rectangle

Trace each **rectangle** and color the picture.

12345

ON   OFF

7 8 9 X
4 5 6 −
1 2 3
0 . = +

33   Denver International SchoolHouse

Rectangle

Name:_____

Color the **rectangles**.

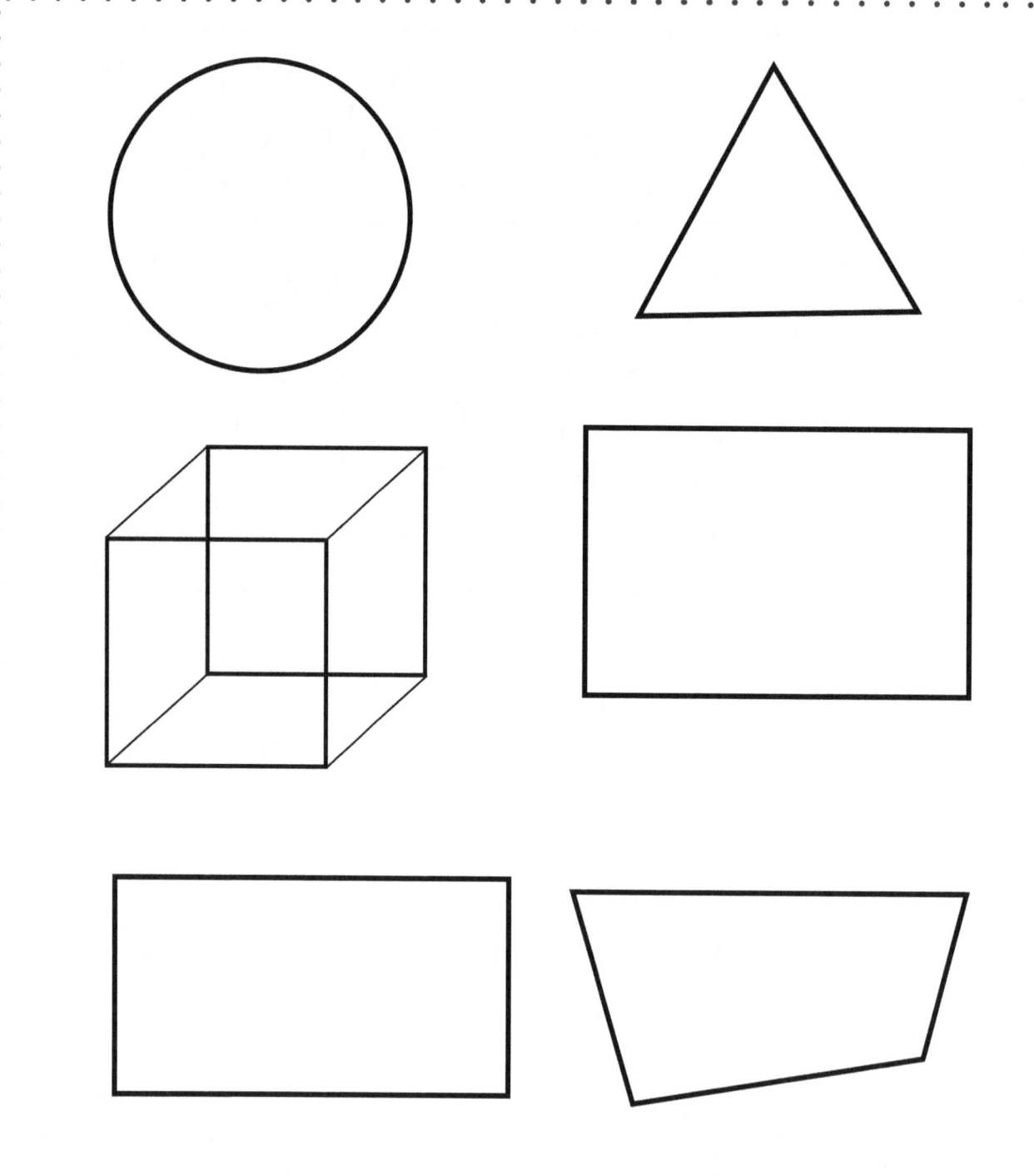

Denver International SchoolHouse 34

Name:_____

Trace, color and write

Trace and color each **rectangle** with the correct crayon.

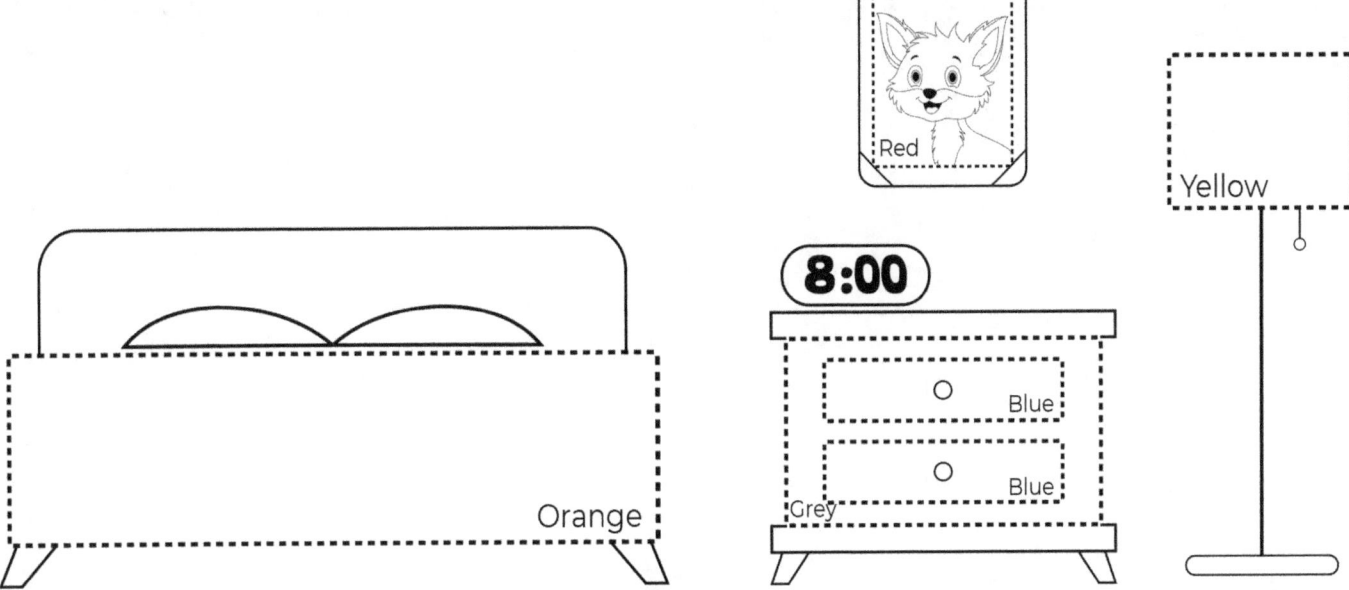

Read the word. Trace the word. Then, write the word on your own.

| rectangle | rectangle |

Name:_____

Rectangle

*Practice drawing **rectangles**.*

*Practice writing **rectangle** on your own.*

Name:_____

Pentagon

Trace the **pentagons**.

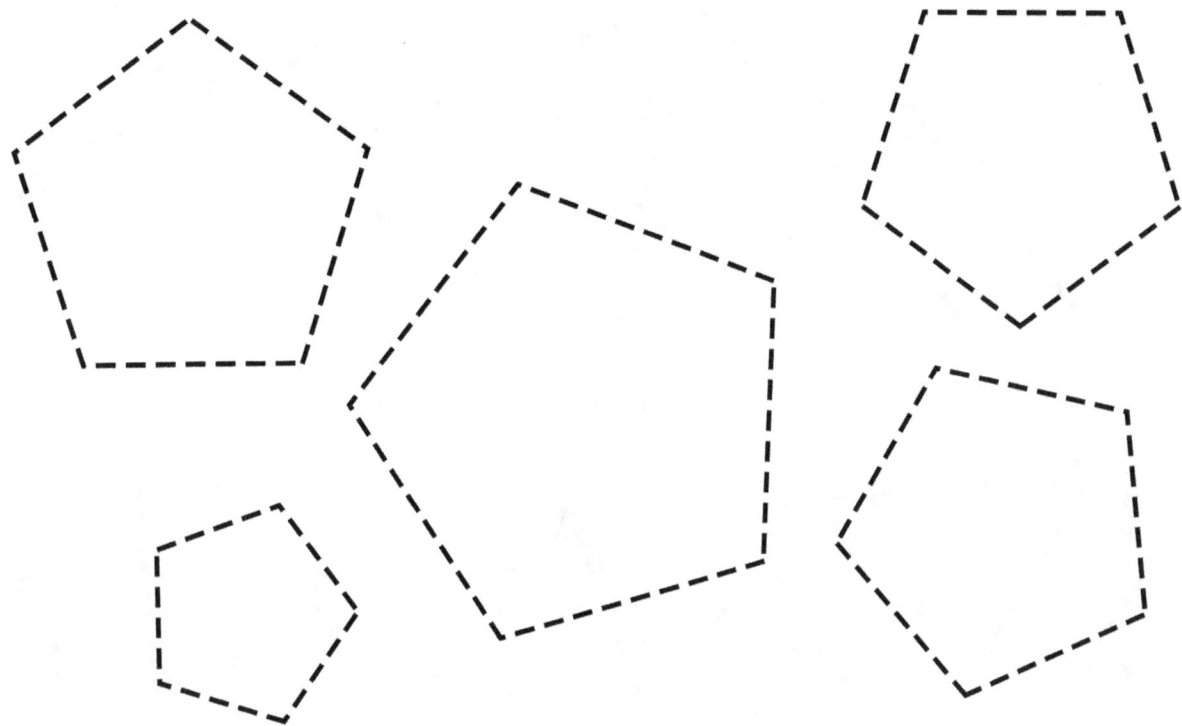

Trace the word.

pentagon

Name:_____

Pentagon

Trace the **pentagons**.

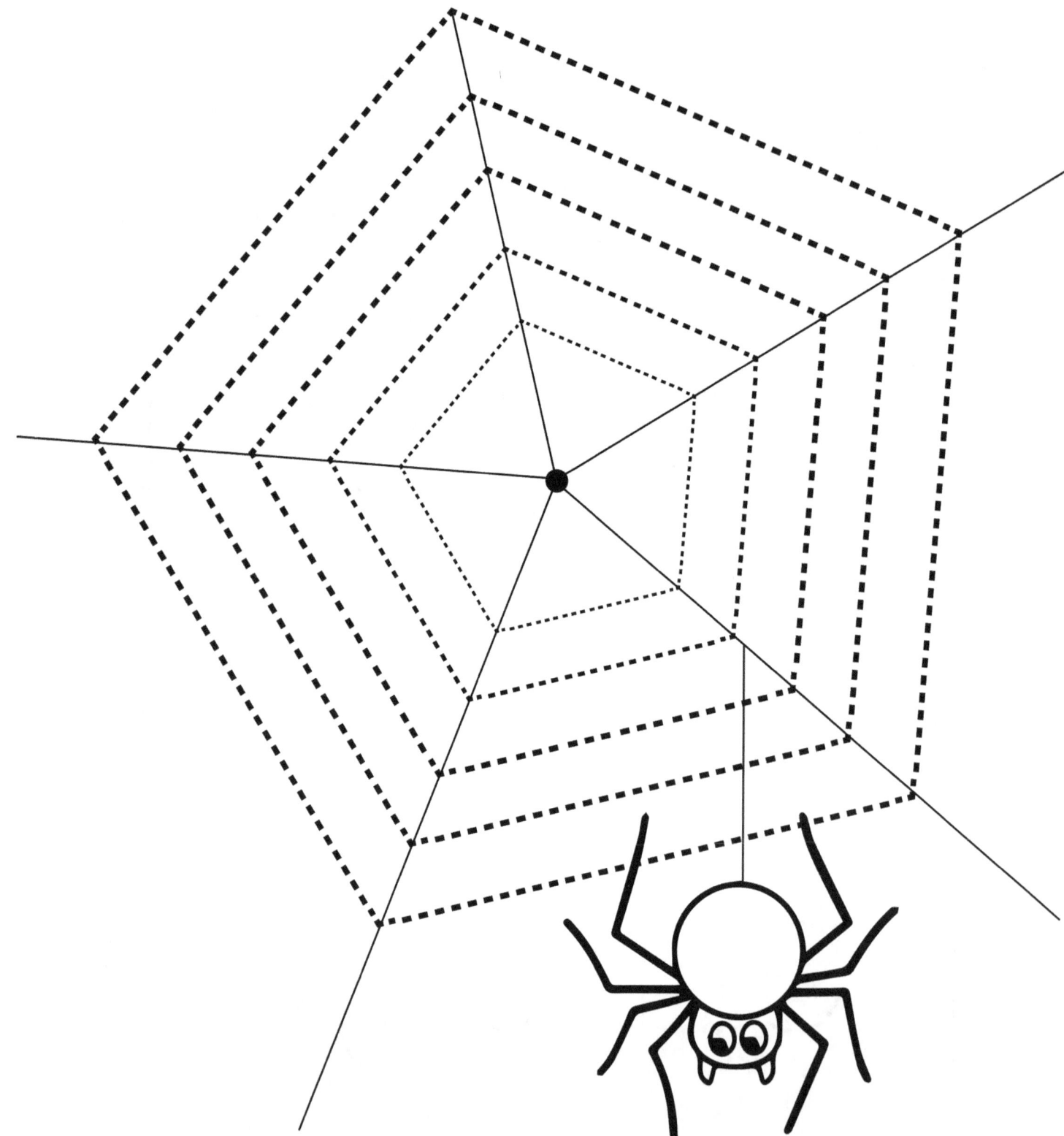

Denver International SchoolHouse

Name:_____

Pentagon

Trace each **pentagon** and color the picture.

Name:_____

Pentagon

Color the **pentagons**.

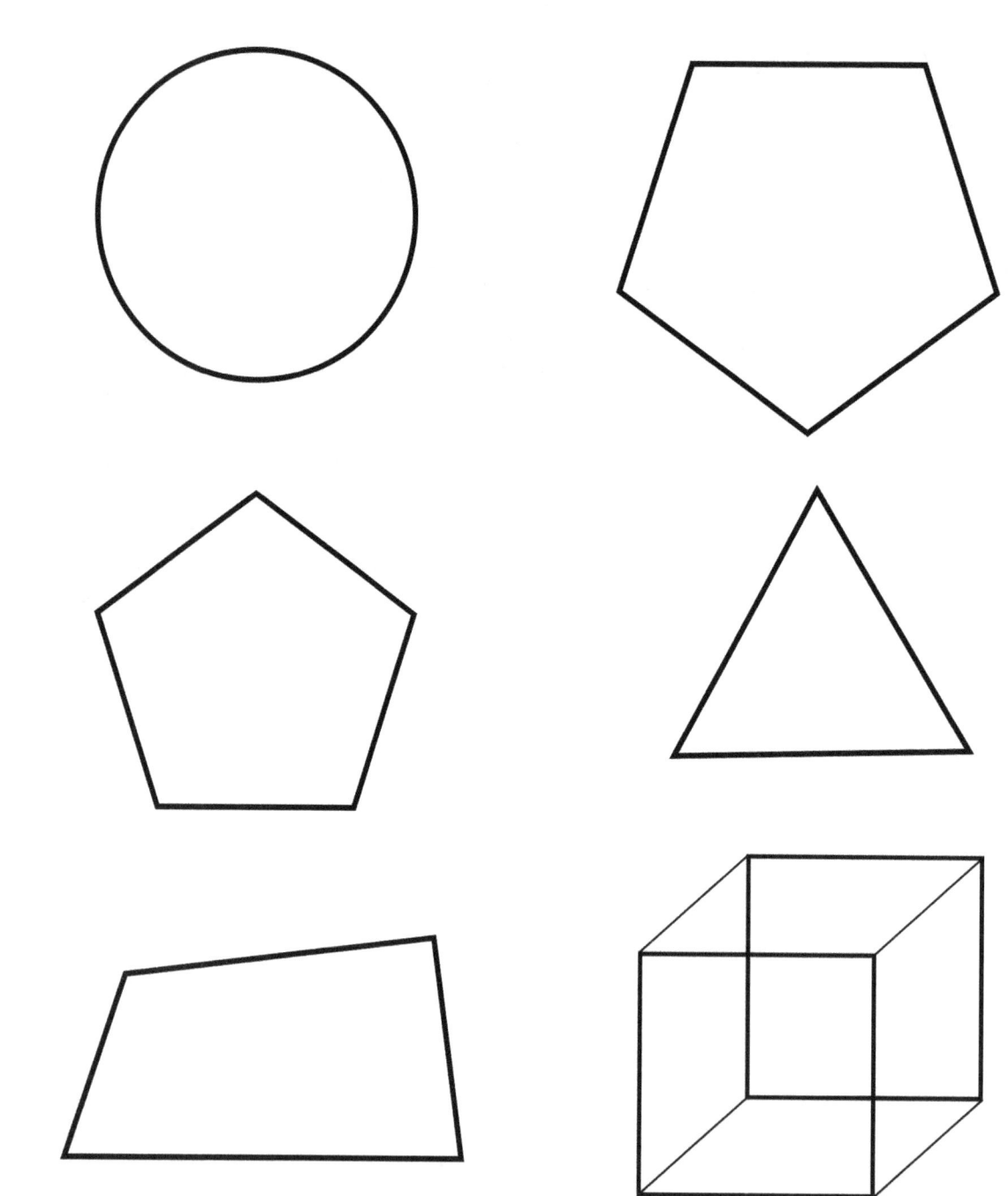

Name:_____

Trace, color and write

Trace and color each **pentagon** with the correct crayon.

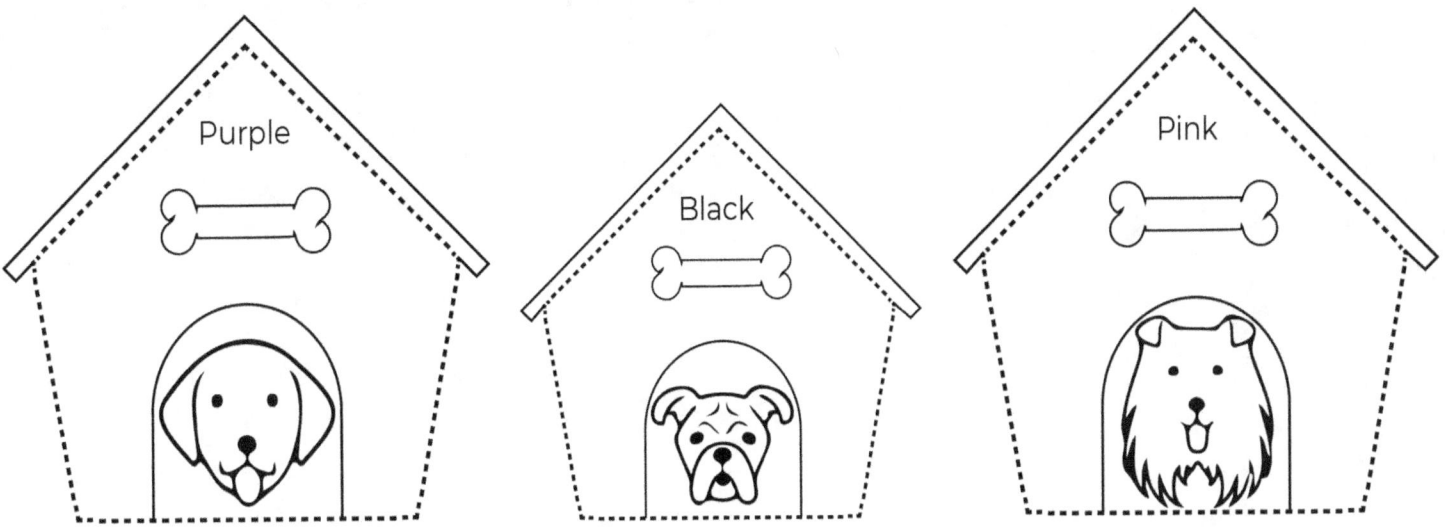

Read the word. Trace the word. Then, write the word on your own.

| pentagon | pentagon |

Name:_____

Pentagon

*Practice drawing **pentagons**.*

*Practice writing **pentagon** on your own.*

Name:_____

Star

Trace the **stars**.

Trace the word.

star

Name:_____

Star

Trace the *stars*.

Name:_____

Star

Trace each *star* and color the picture.

Name:_____

Star

Color the *stars*.

Name:_____

Trace, color and write

Trace and color each *star* with the correct crayon.

Read the word. Trace the word. Then, write the word on your own.

| star | star |

Denver International SchoolHouse

Name:_____

Star

*Practice drawing **stars**.*

*Practice writing **star** on your own.*

Denver International SchoolHouse

Name:_____

Hexagon

Trace the **hexagons**.

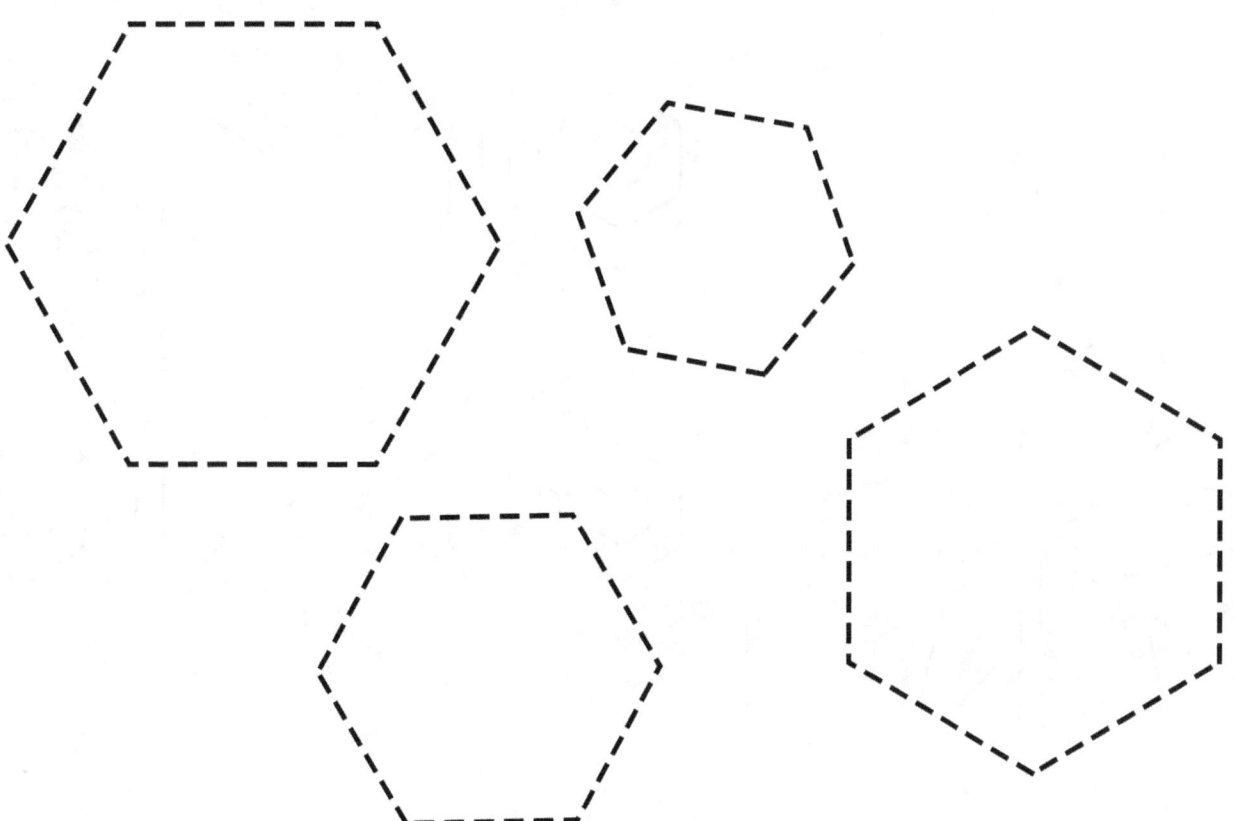

Trace the word.

hexagon

Hexagon

Name:_____

Trace the **hexagons**.

Name:_____

Hexagon

Trace each **hexagon** and color the picture.

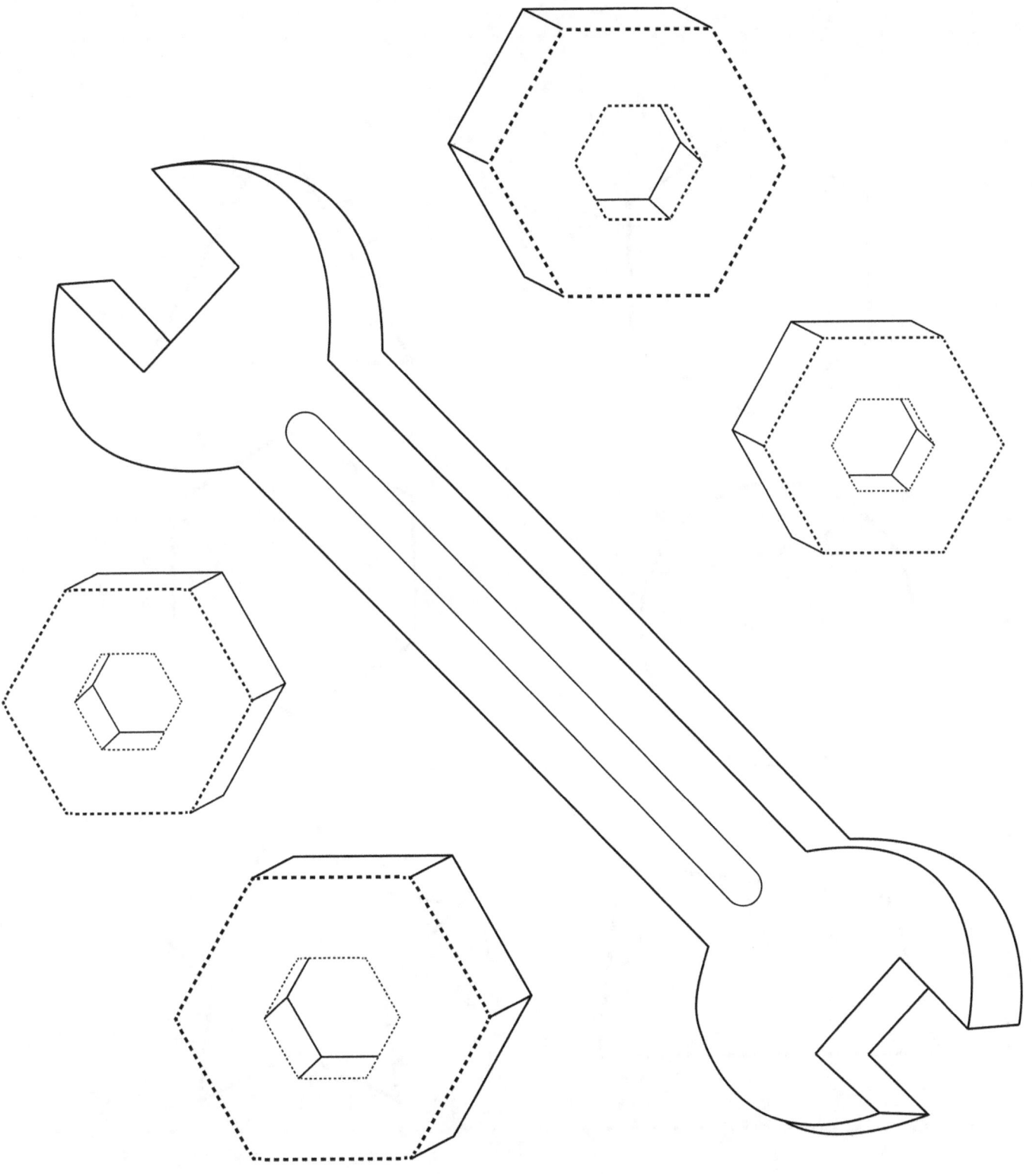

51   Denver International SchoolHouse

Name:_____

Hexagon

Color the **hexagons**.

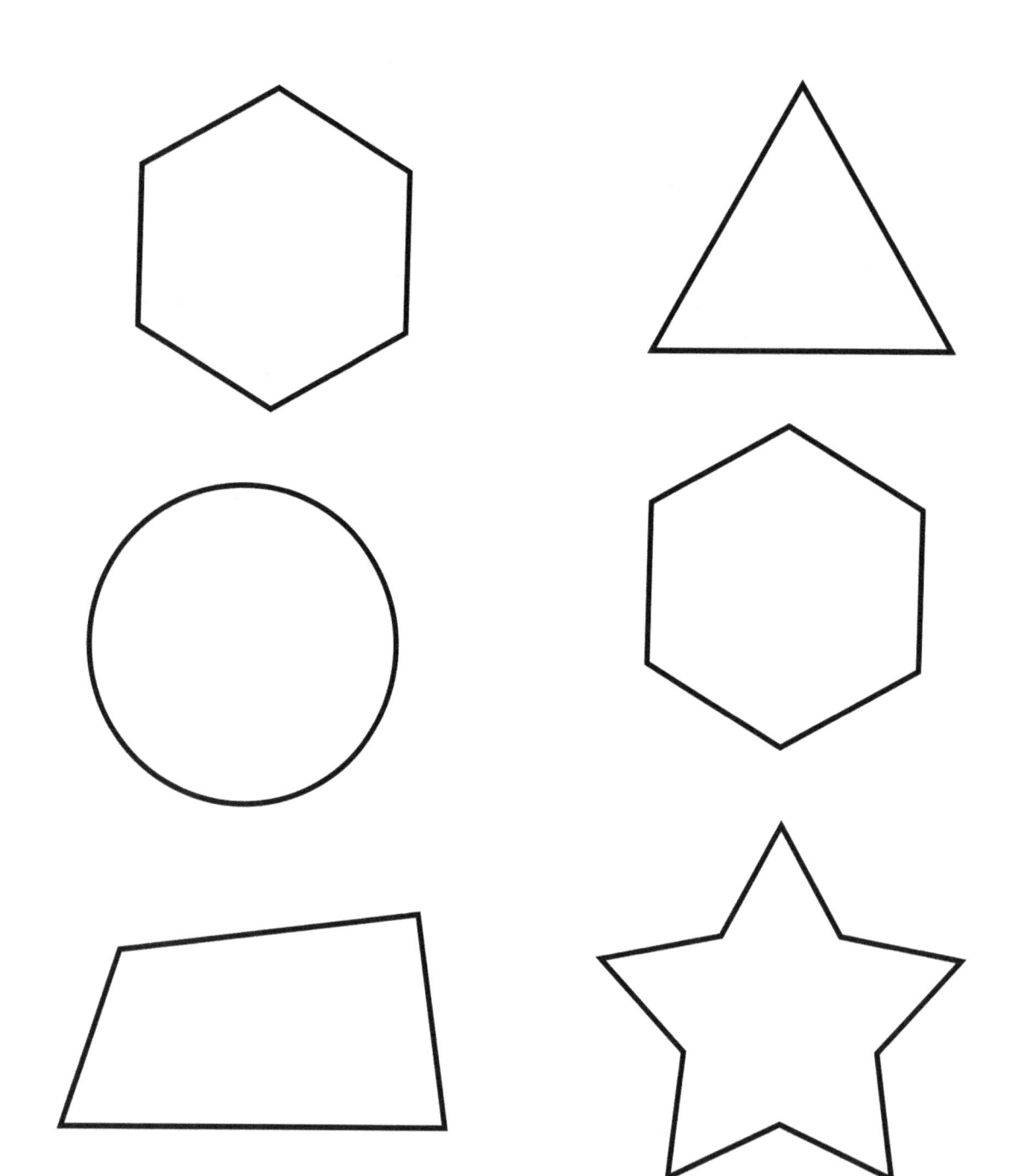

Name:_____

Trace, color and write

Trace and color each **hexagon** with the correct crayon.

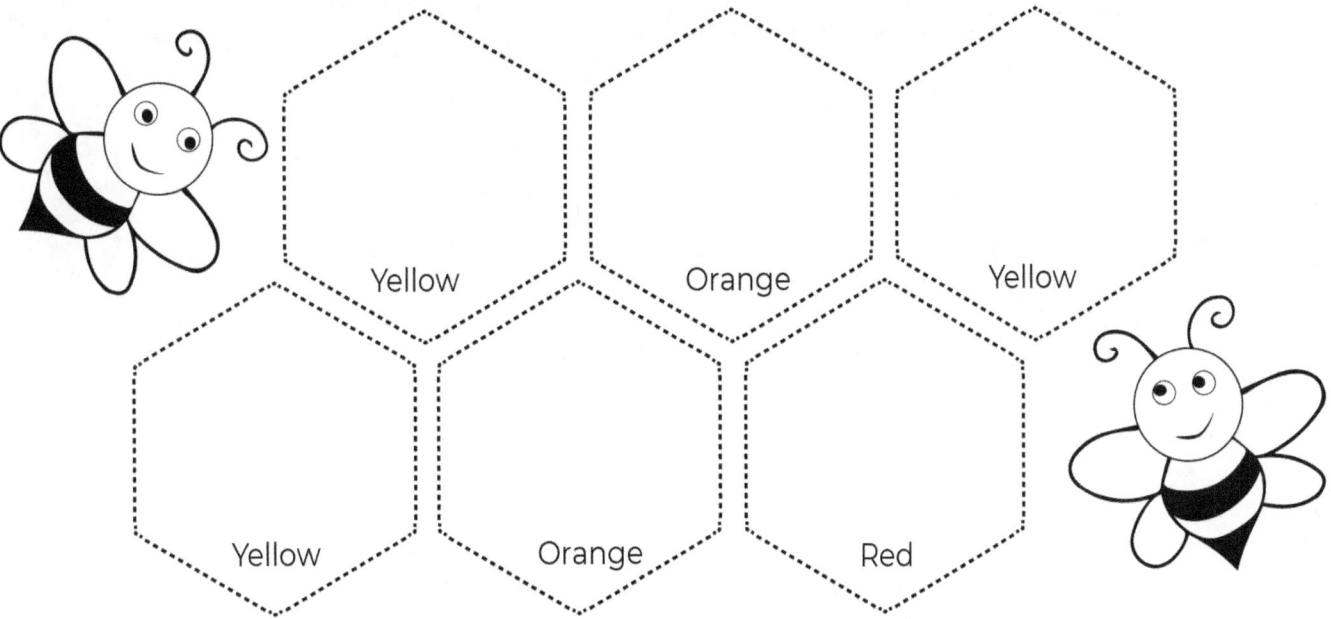

Read the word. Trace the word. Then, write the word on your own.

hexagon | hexagon

Name:_____

Hexagon

*Practice drawing **hexagons**.*

*Practice writing **hexagon** on your own.*

Denver International SchoolHouse

Name:_____

Diamond

Trace the **diamonds**.

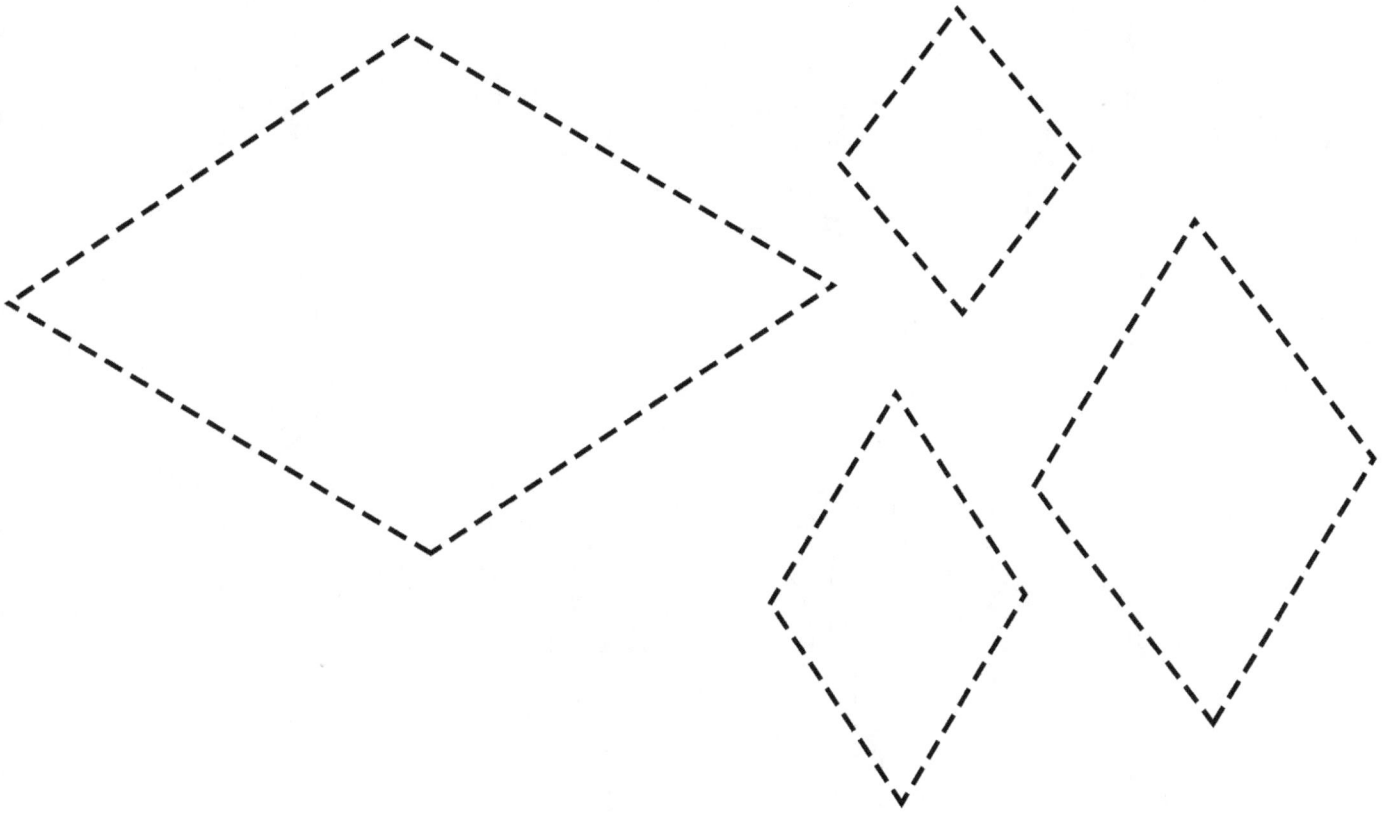

Trace the word.

diamond

Name:_____

Diamond

Trace the **diamonds**.

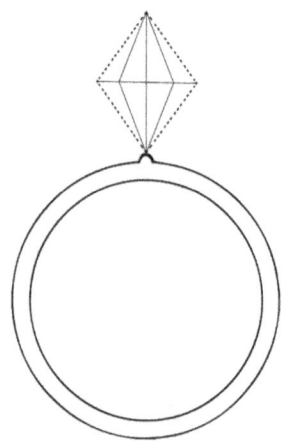
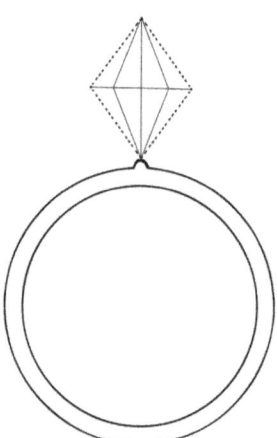
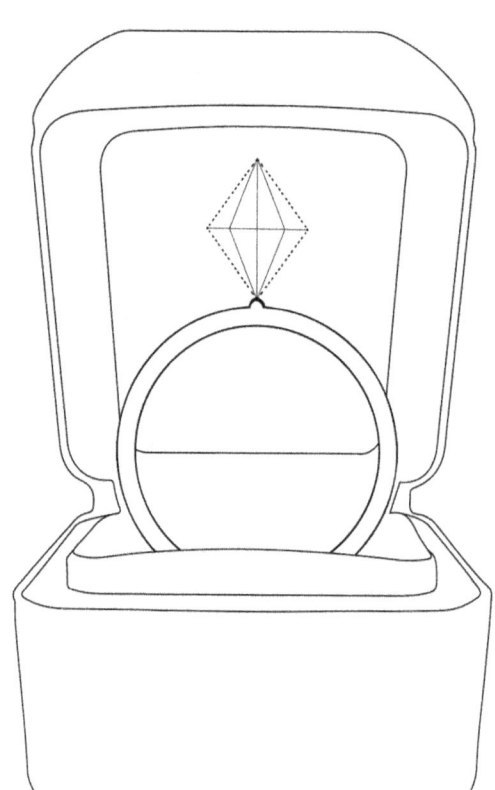
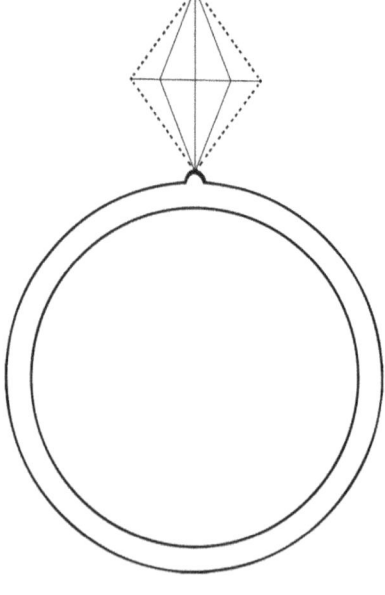
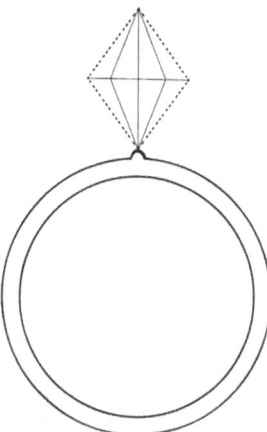

Diamond

Trace each **diamond** and color the picture.

Name:_____

Diamond

Color the **diamond**.

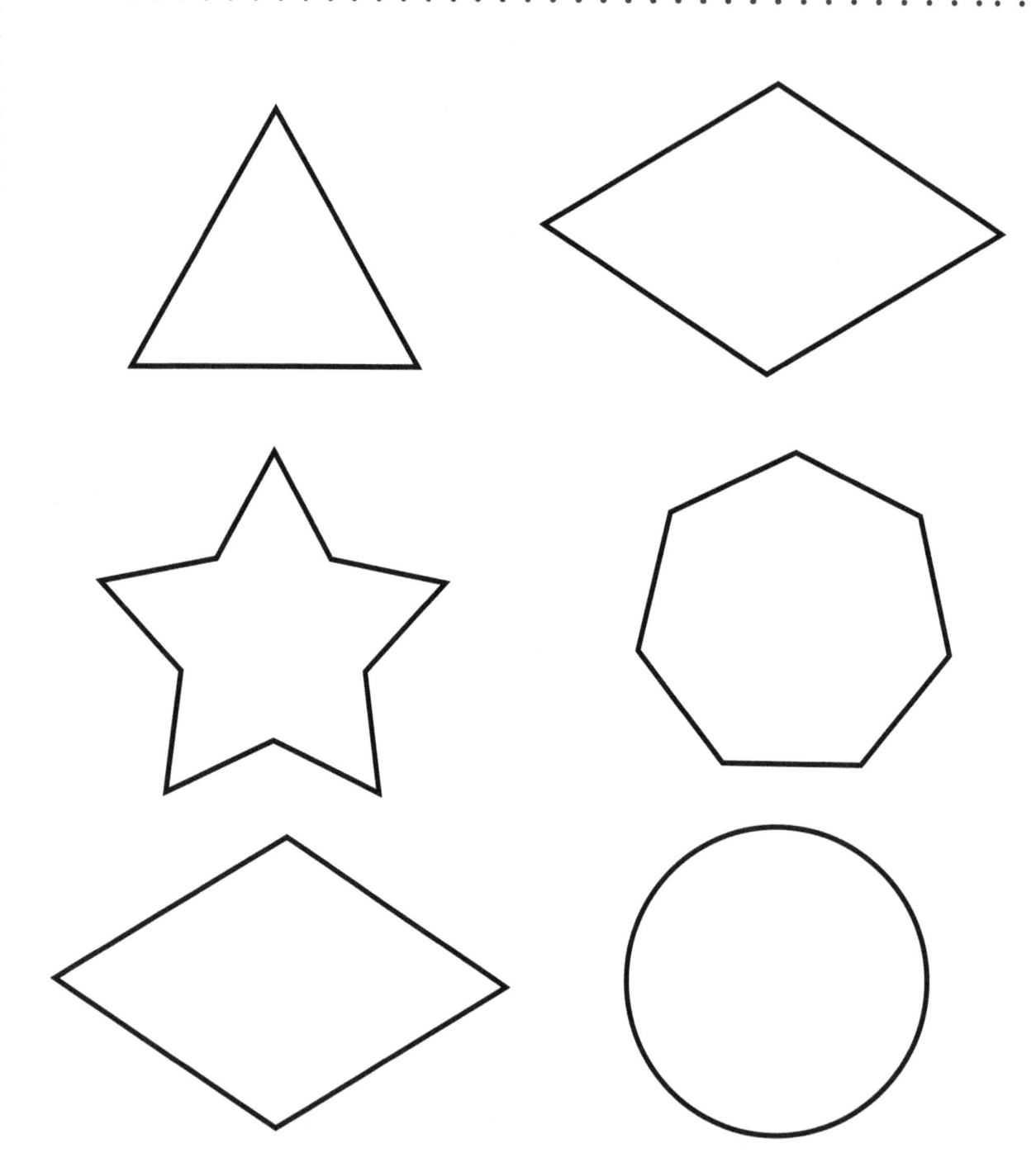

Denver International SchoolHouse

Name:_____

Trace, color and write

Trace and color each **diamond** with the correct crayon.

Read the word. Trace the word. Then, write the word on your own.

| diamond | diamond |

Name:_____

Diamond

*Practice drawing **diamonds**.*

*Practice writing **diamond** on your own.*

Denver International SchoolHouse

Name:_____

Heptagon

Trace the **heptagons**.

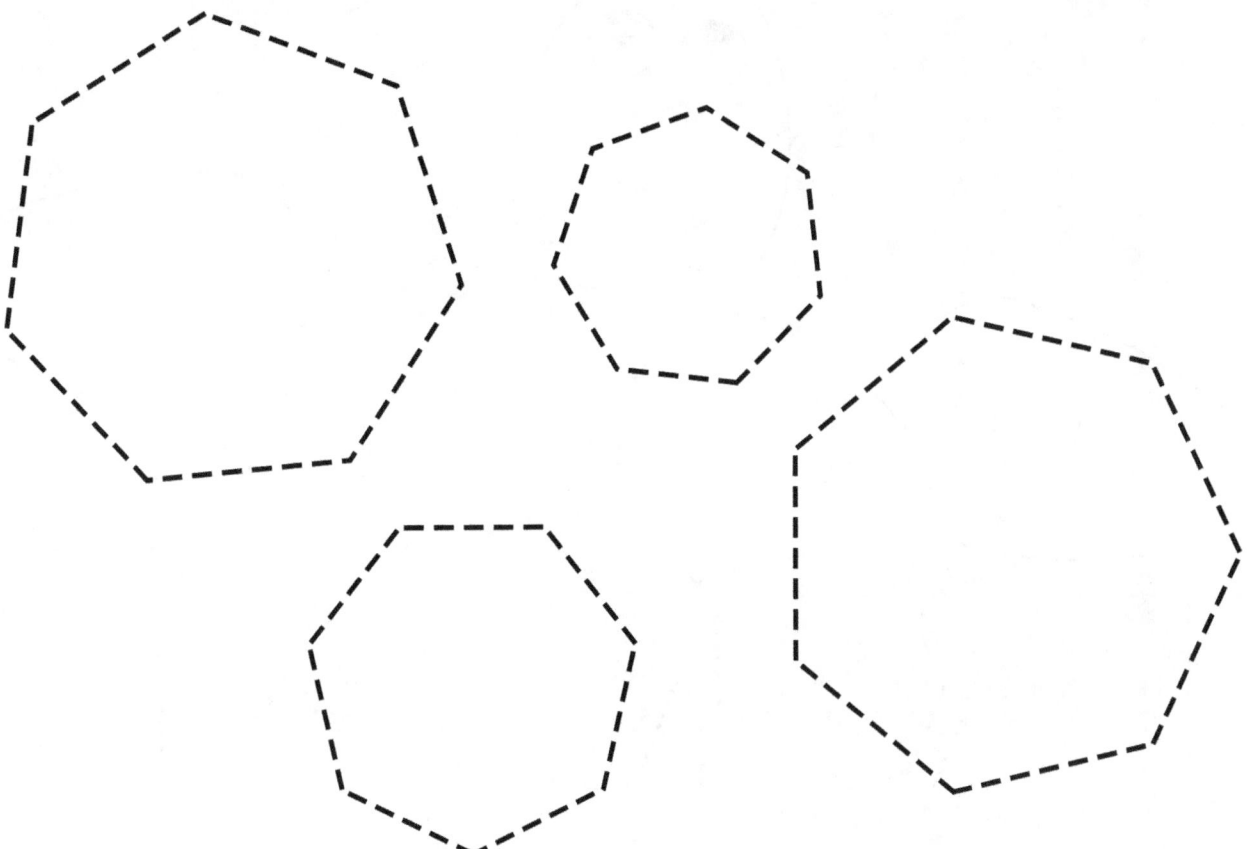

Trace the word.

heptagon

Heptagon

Name:_____

Trace the **heptagons**.

Denver International SchoolHouse

Name:_____

Heptagon

Trace each **heptagon** and color the picture.

Heptagon

Name:_____

Color the **heptagon**.

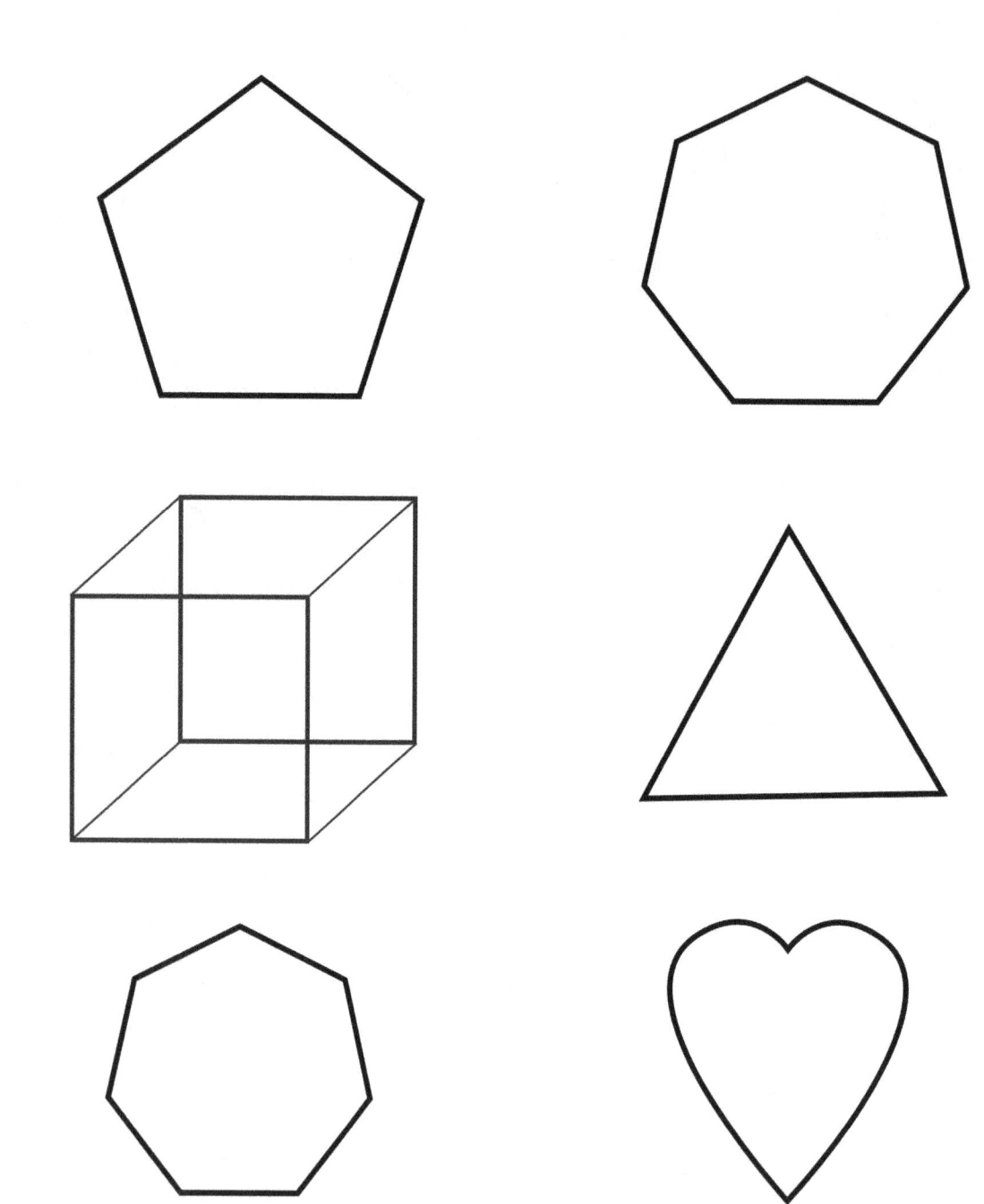

Denver International SchoolHouse

Name:_____

Trace, color and write

Trace and color each **heptagon** with the correct crayon.

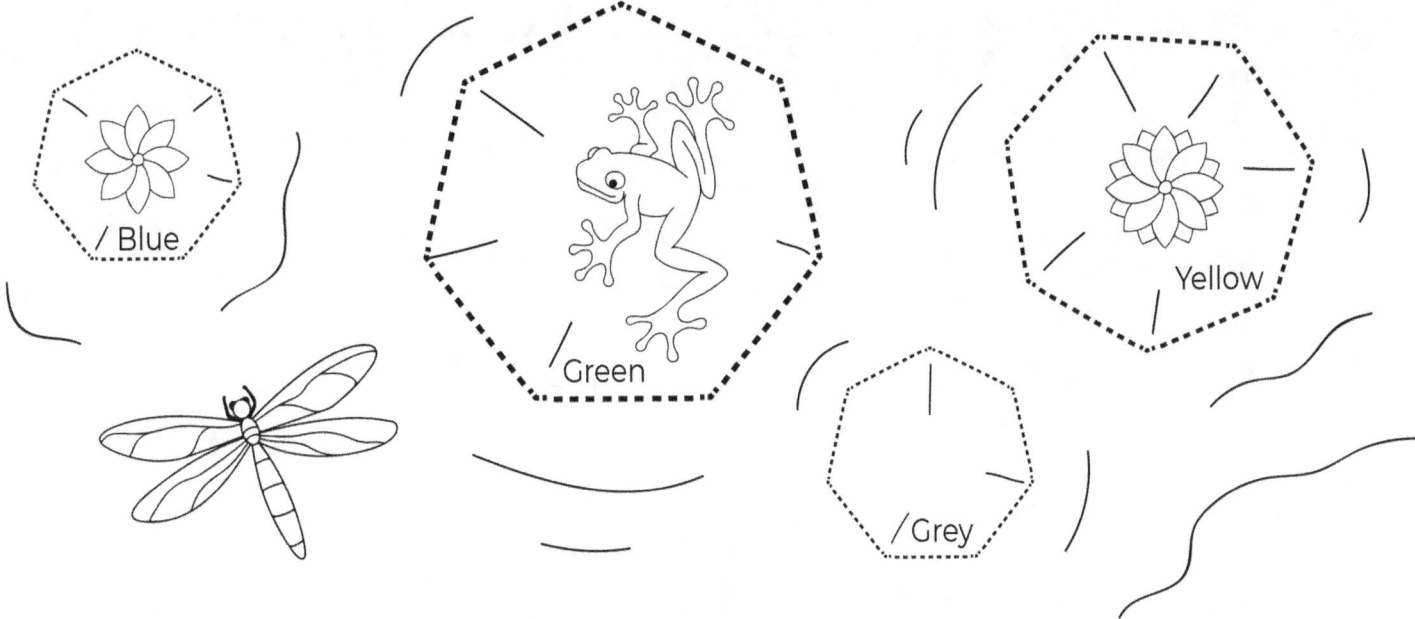

Read the word. Trace the word. Then, write the word on your own.

heptagon | heptagon

Name:_____

Heptagon

Practice drawing **heptagons**.

Practice writing **heptagon** *on your own.*

Name:_____

Heart

Trace the **hearts**.

Trace the word.

Name:_____

Heart

Trace the hearts.

Denver International SchoolHouse

Name:_____

Heart

Trace each *heart* and color the picture.

69 Denver International SchoolHouse

Heart

Name:_____

Color the **heart**.

Name:_____

Trace, color and write

Trace and color each **heart** with the correct crayon.

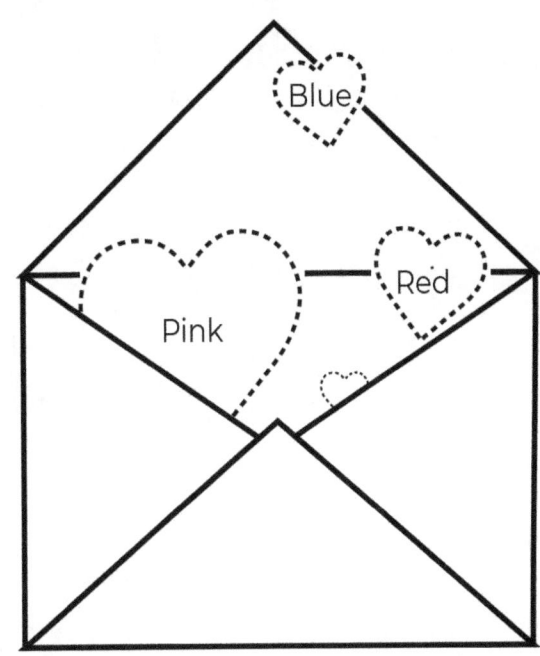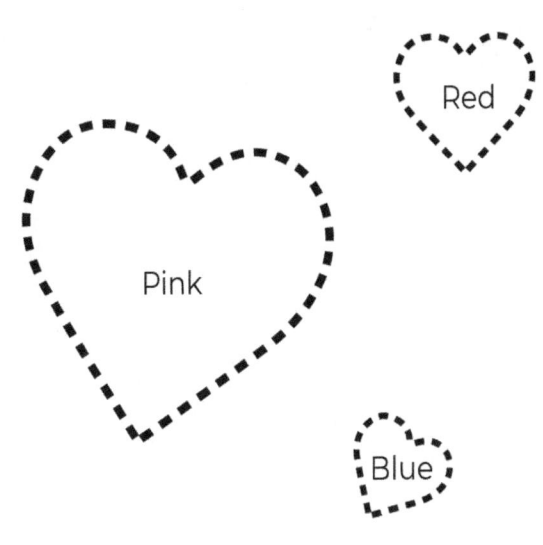

Read the word. Trace the word. Then, write the word on your own.

| heart | heart |

71 Denver International SchoolHouse

Name:_____

Heart

*Practice drawing **hearts**.*

*Practice writing **heart** on your own.*

Denver International SchoolHouse

Name:_____

Octagon

Trace the **octagons**.

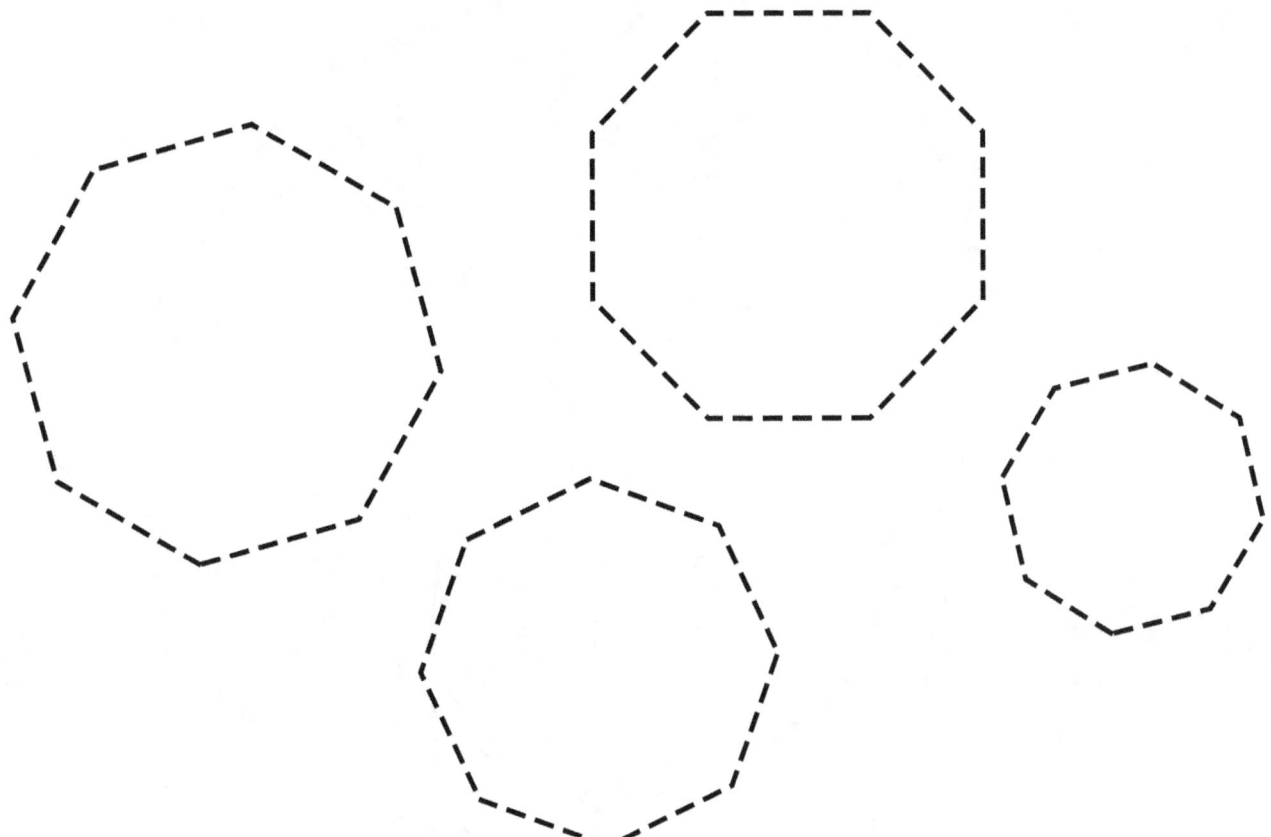

Trace the word.

octagon

Name:_____

Octagon

Trace the **octagons**.

Name:_____

Octagon

Trace each **octagon** and color the picture.

Name:_____

Octagon

Color the **octagons**.

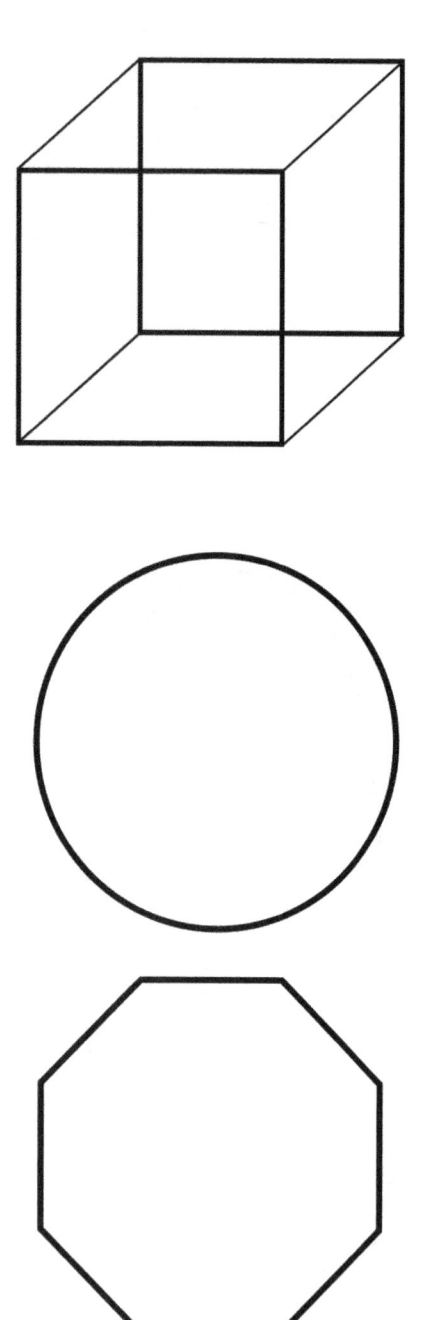
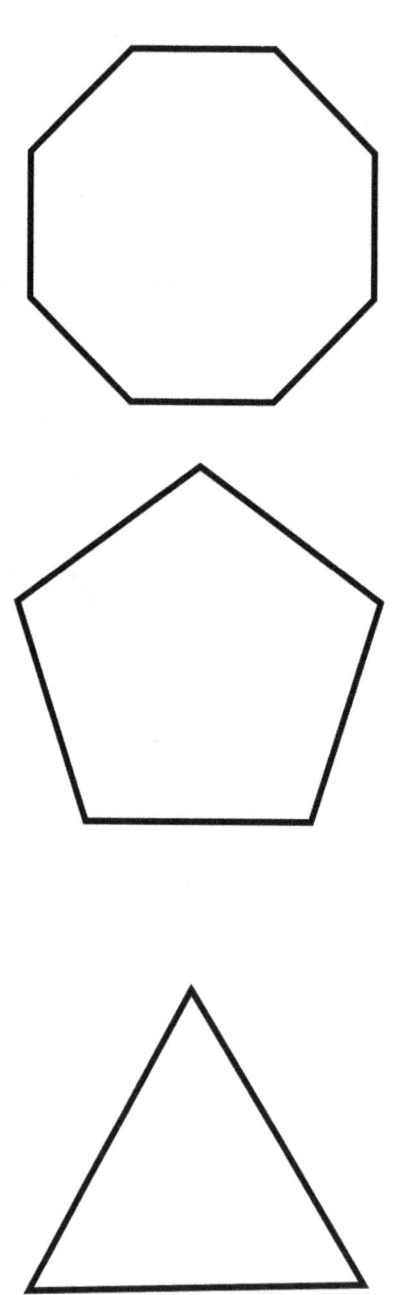

Name:_____

Trace, color and write

Trace and color each **octagon** with the correct crayon.

Read the word. Trace the word. Then, write the word on your own.

octagon | octagon

77 Denver International SchoolHouse

Name:_____

Octagon

*Practice drawing **octagons**.*

*Practice writing **octagon** on your own.*

Denver International SchoolHouse

Name:_____

Pyramid

Trace the **pyramids**.

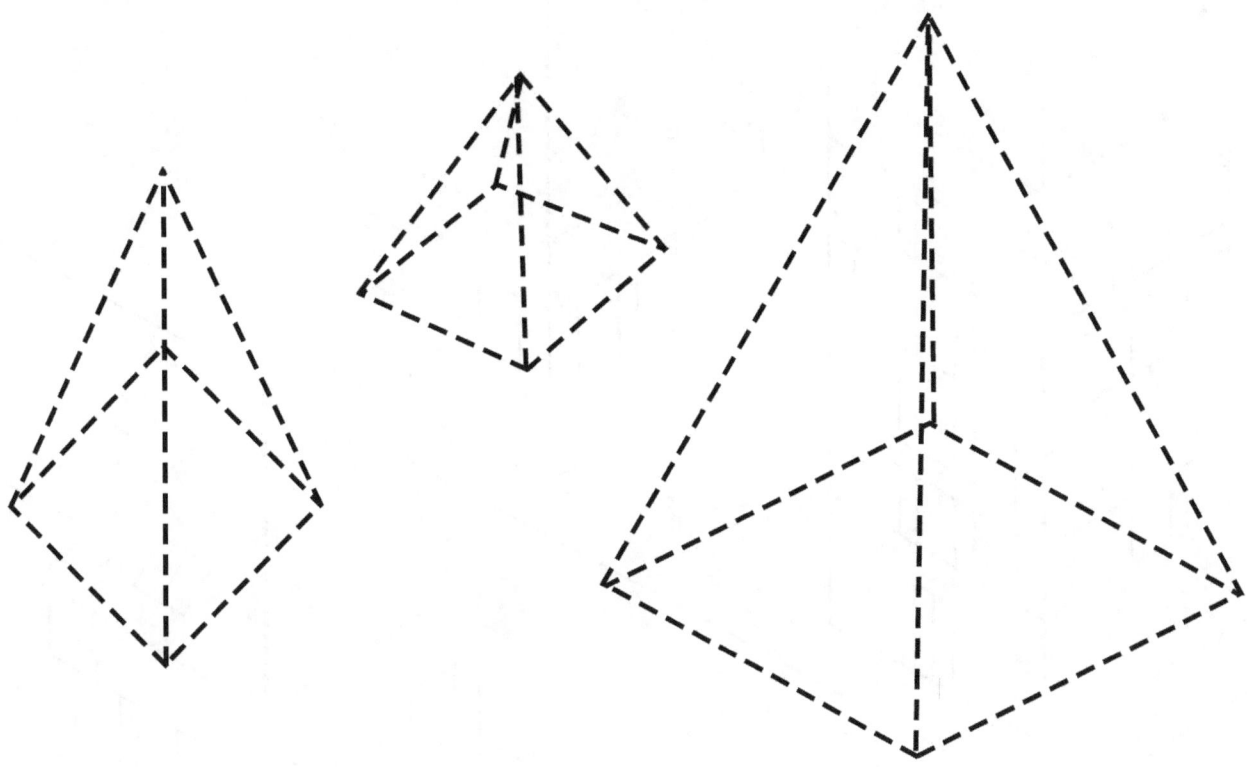

Trace the word.

pyramid

Pyramid

Name:_____

Trace the **pyramids**.

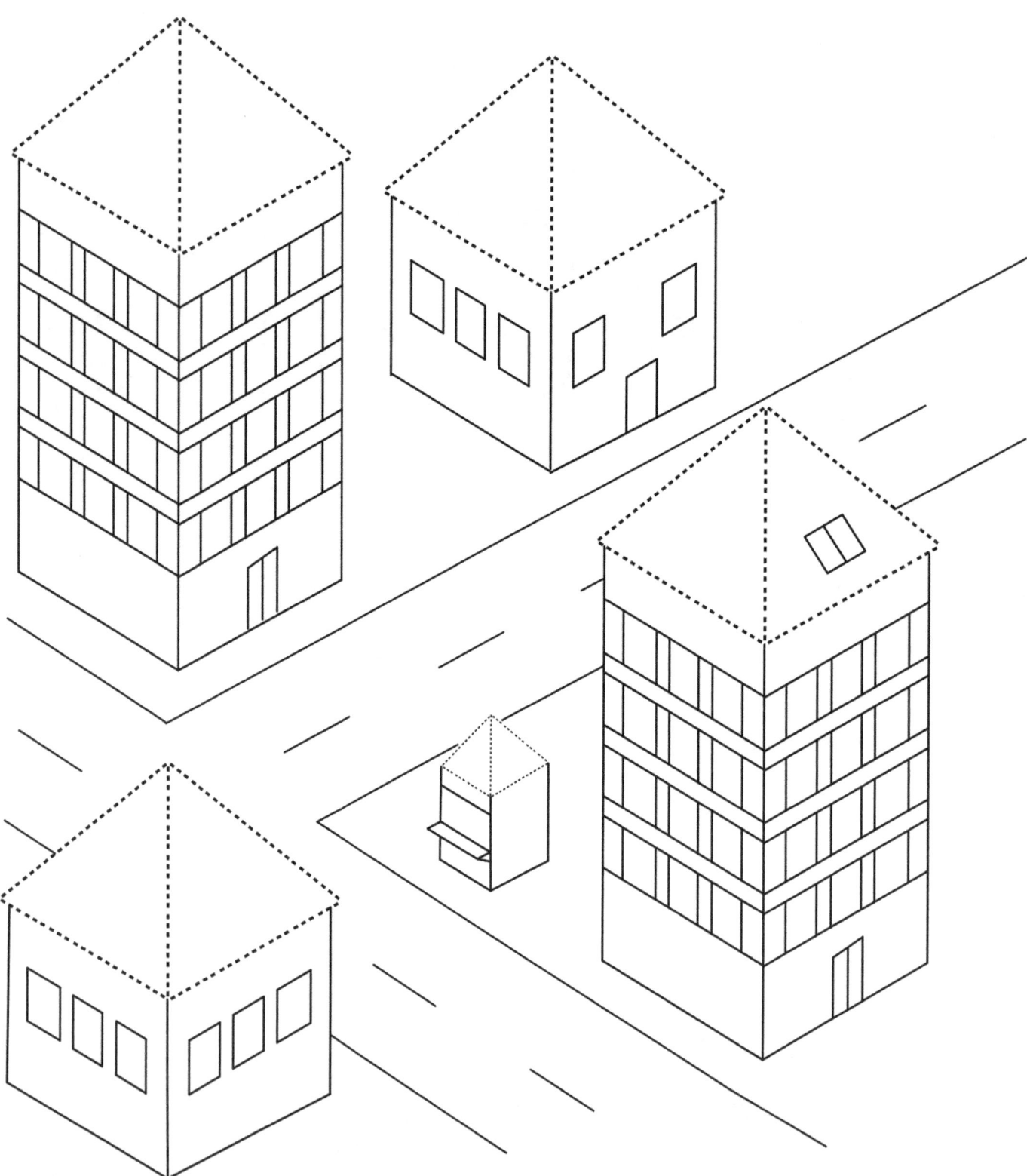

Denver International SchoolHouse

Name:_____

Pyramid

Trace each **pyramid** and color the picture.

Name:_____

Pyramid

Color the **pyramids**.

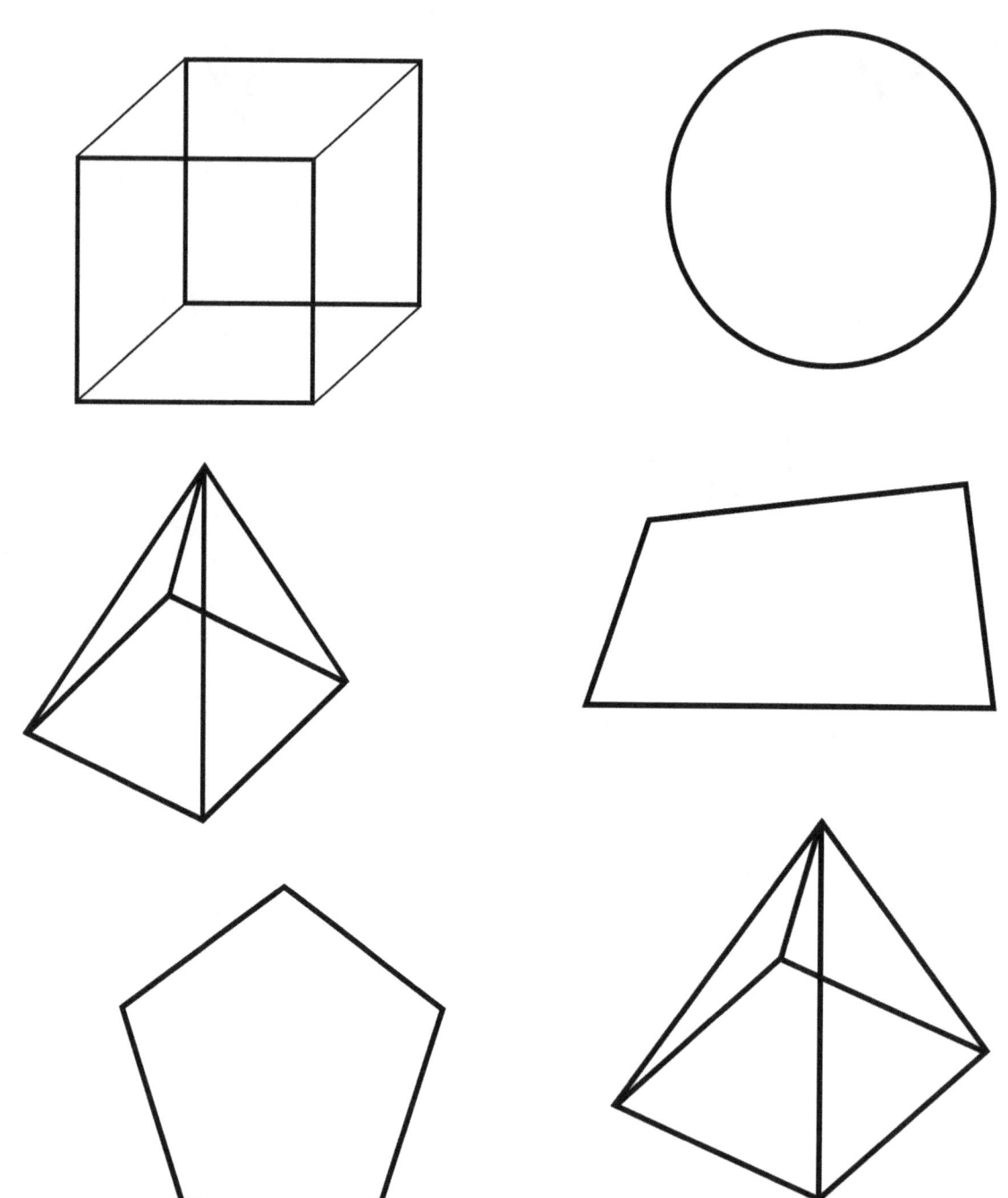

Name:_____

Trace, color and write

Trace and color each **pyramid** with the correct crayon.

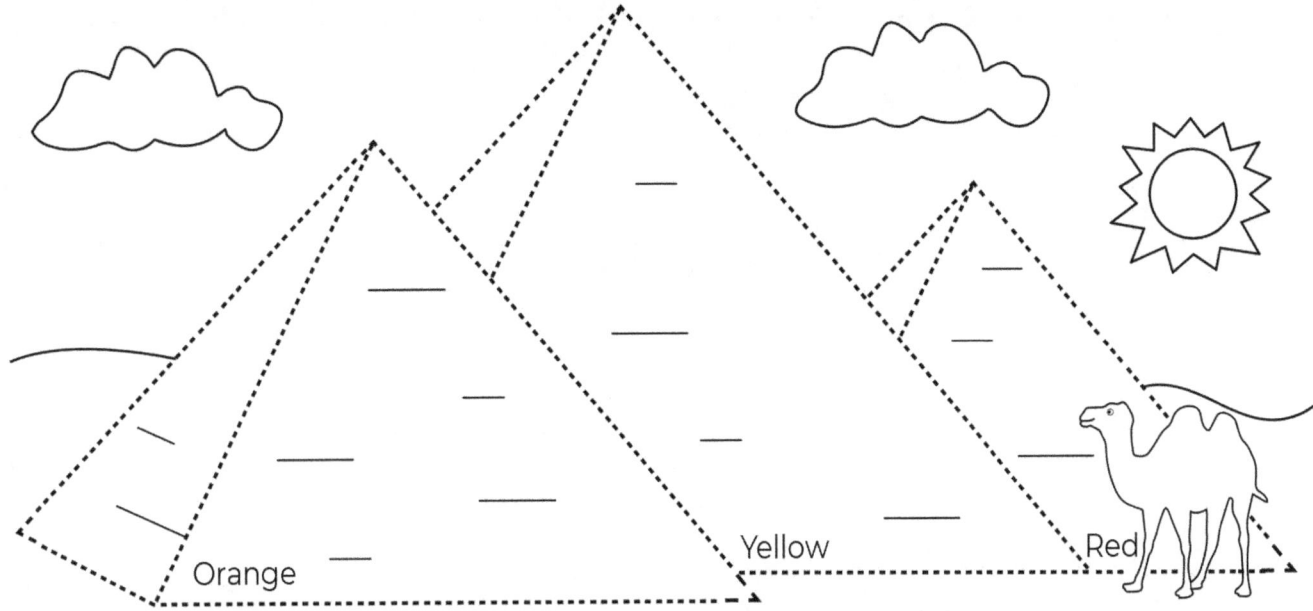

Orange   Yellow   Red

Read the word. Trace the word. Then, write the word on your own.

| pyramid | pyramid |

83   Denver International SchoolHouse

Name:_____

Pyramid

*Practice drawing **pyramids**.*

*Practice writing **pyramid** on your own.*

Denver International SchoolHouse   84

Name:_____

Cone

Trace the **cones**.

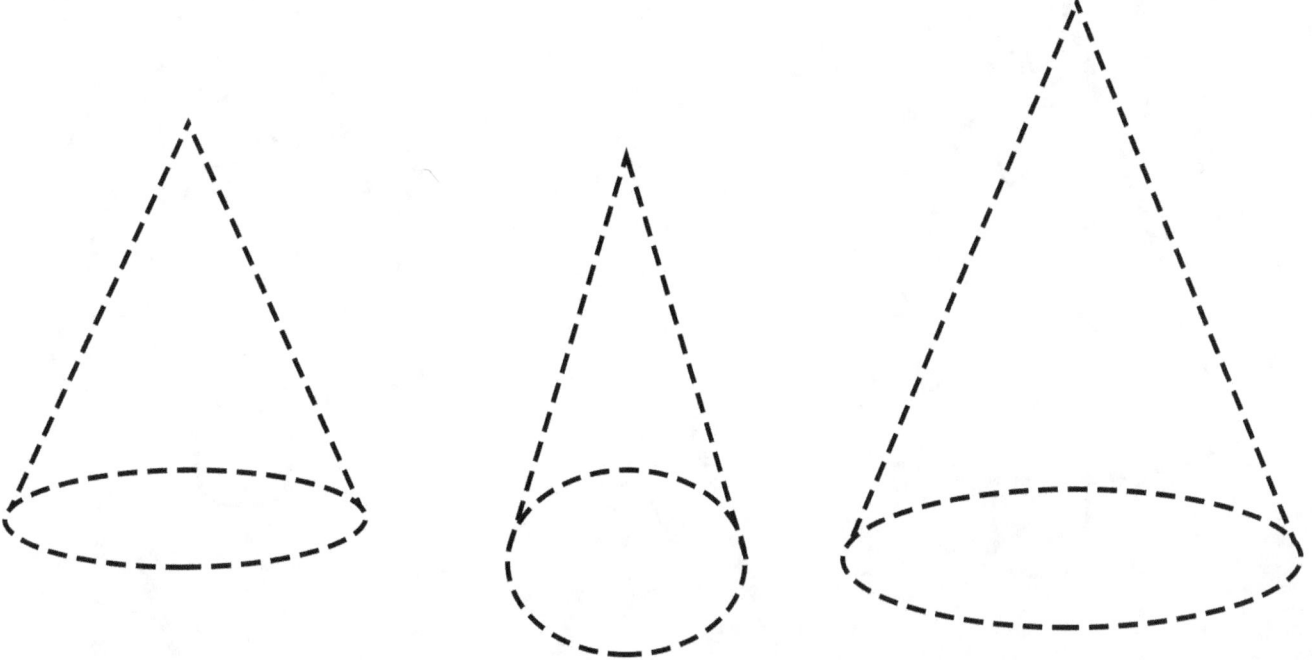

Trace the word.

Name:_____

Cone

Trace the **cones**.

Denver International SchoolHouse

Name:_____

Cone

Trace each **cone** and color the picture.

Name:_____

Cone

Color the **cone**.

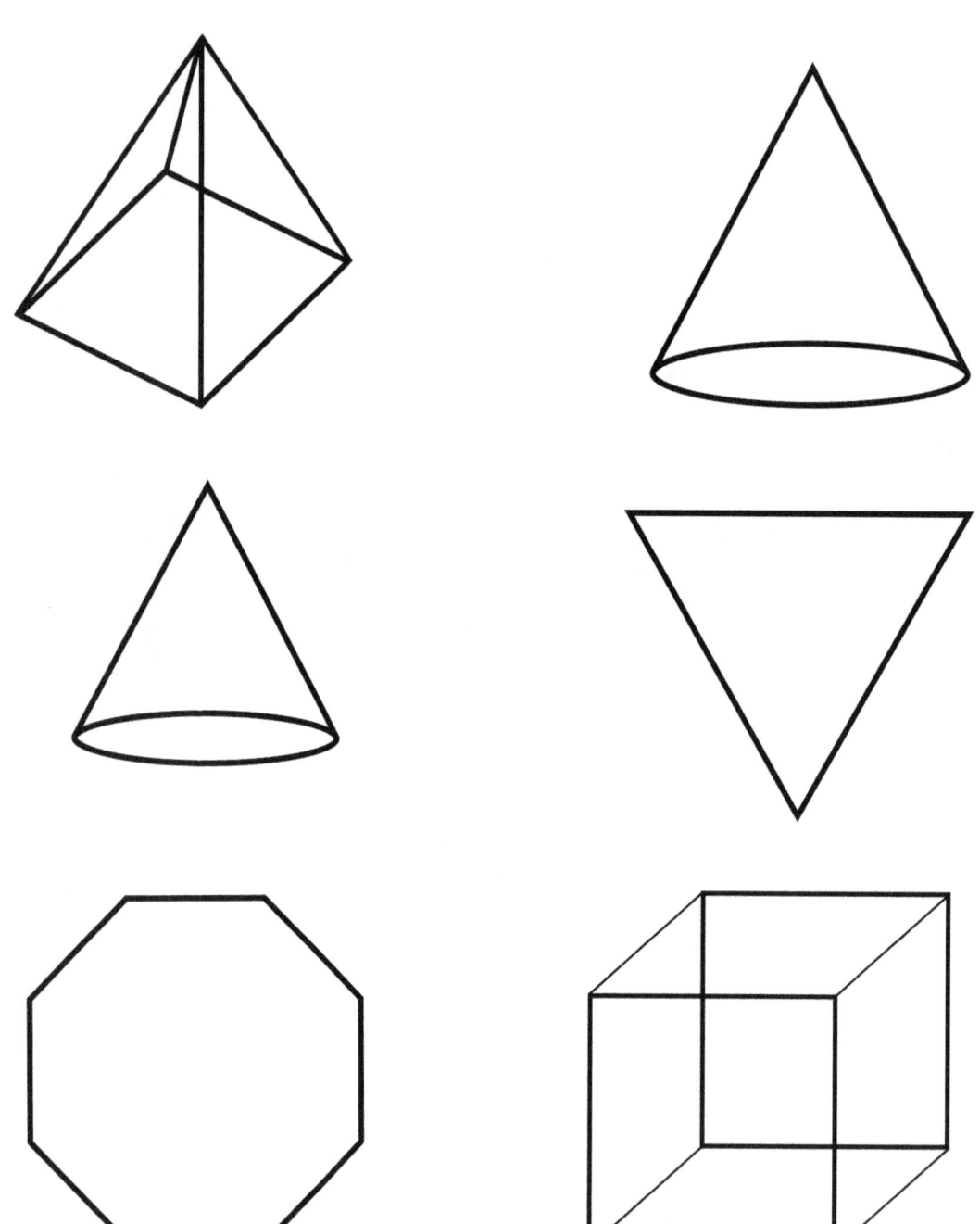

Name:_____

Trace, color and write

Trace and color each **cone** with the correct crayon.

Read the word. Trace the word. Then, write the word on your own.

| cone | cone |

Name:_____

Cone

*Practice drawing **cones**.*

*Practice writing **cone** on your own.*

Denver International SchoolHouse

Name:_____

Oval

Trace the **ovals**.

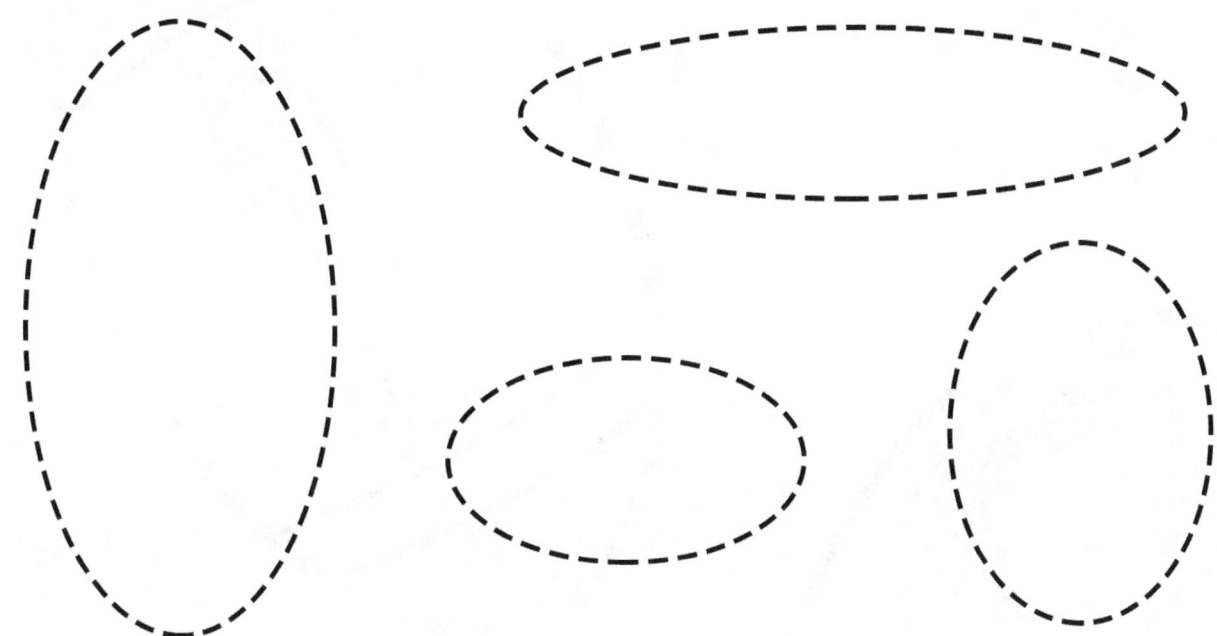

Trace the word.

oval

Name:_____

Oval

Trace the **ovals**.

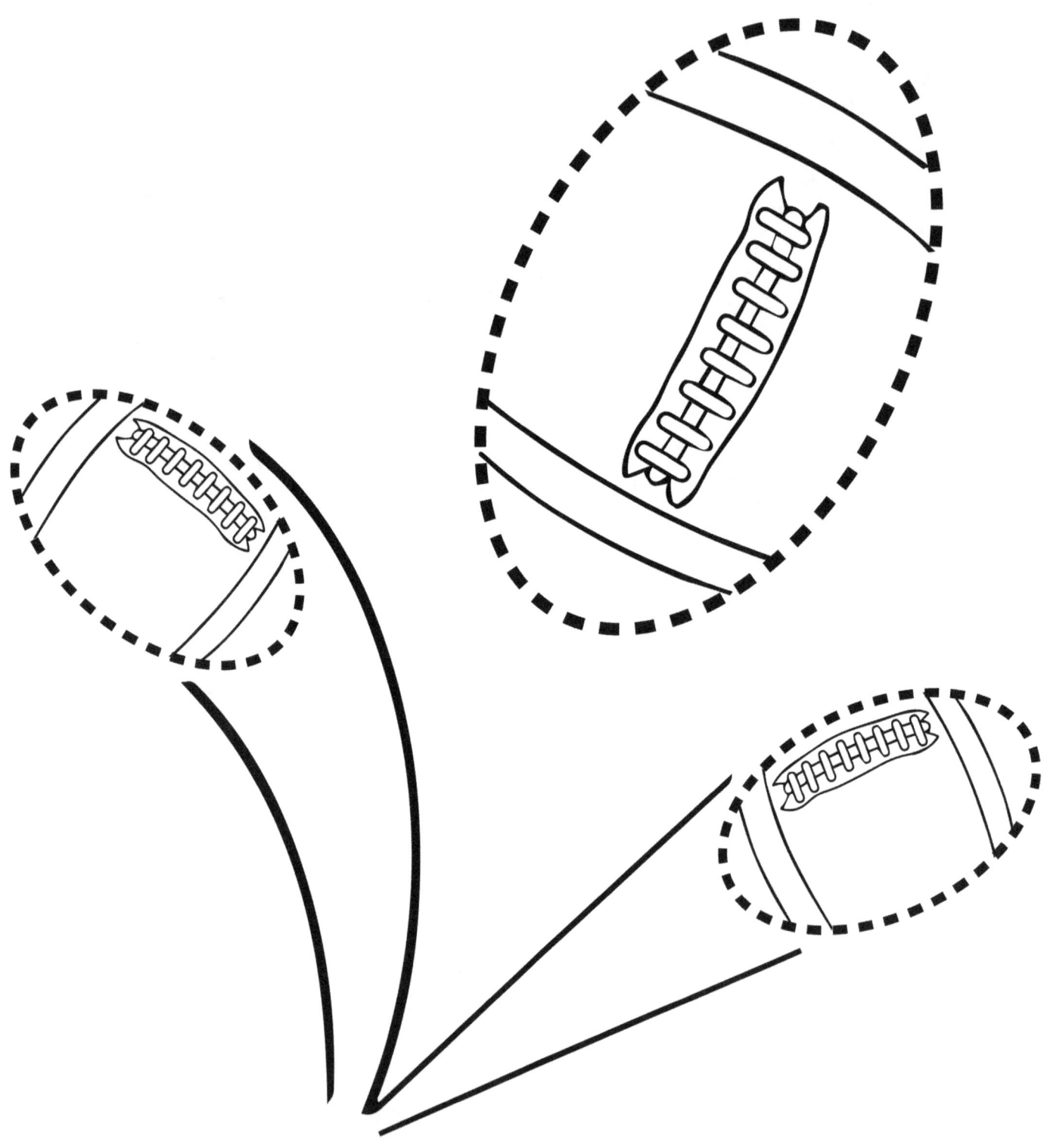

Name:_____

Oval

Trace each **oval** and color the picture.

Oval

Name:_____

Color the **ovals**.

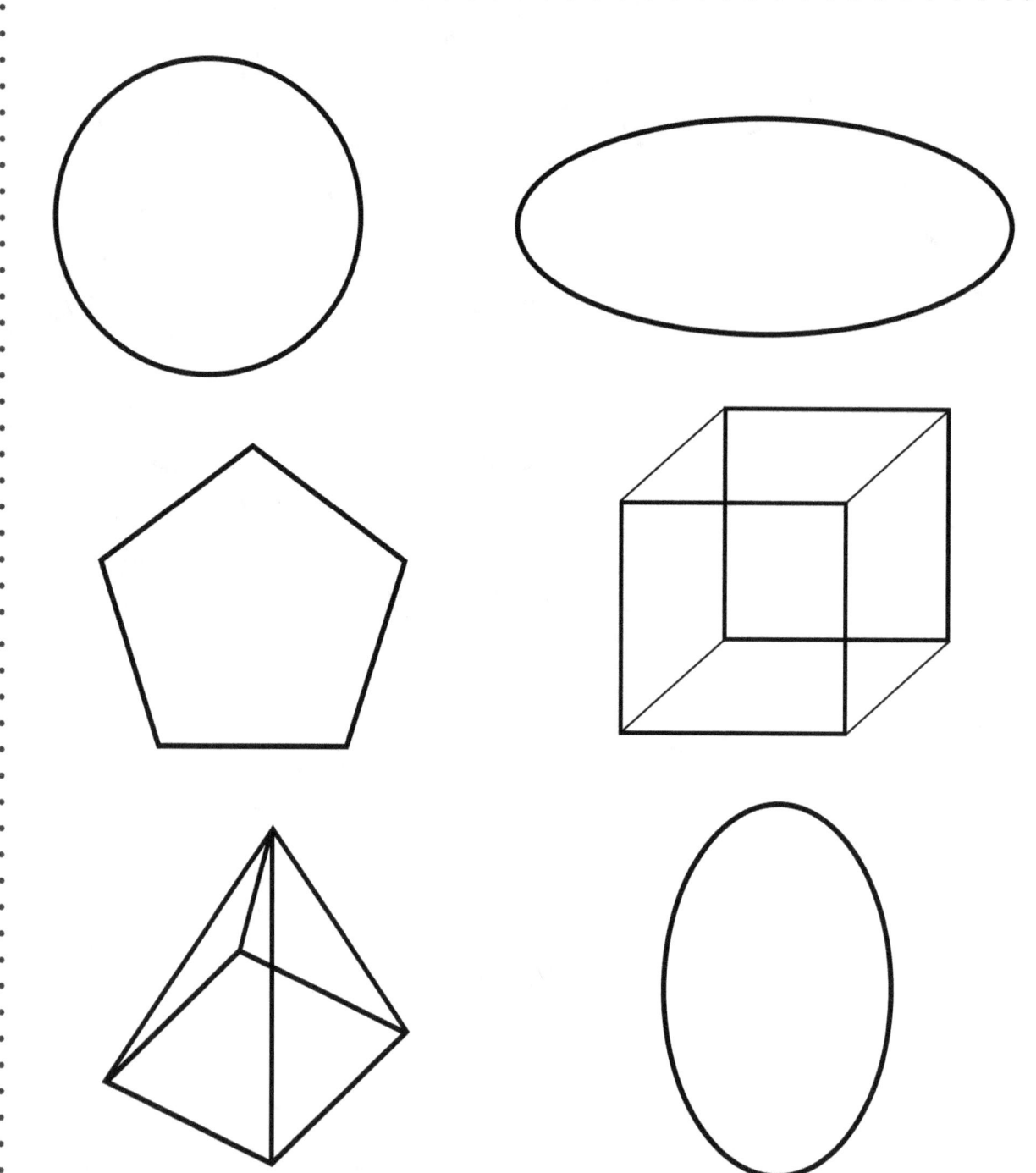

Name:_____

Trace, color and write

Trace and color each **oval** with the correct crayon.

Read the word. Trace the word. Then, write the word on your own.

oval

oval

Name:_____

Oval

Practice drawing **ovals**.

Practice writing **oval** on your own.

Name:_____

Cylinder

Trace the **cylinders**.

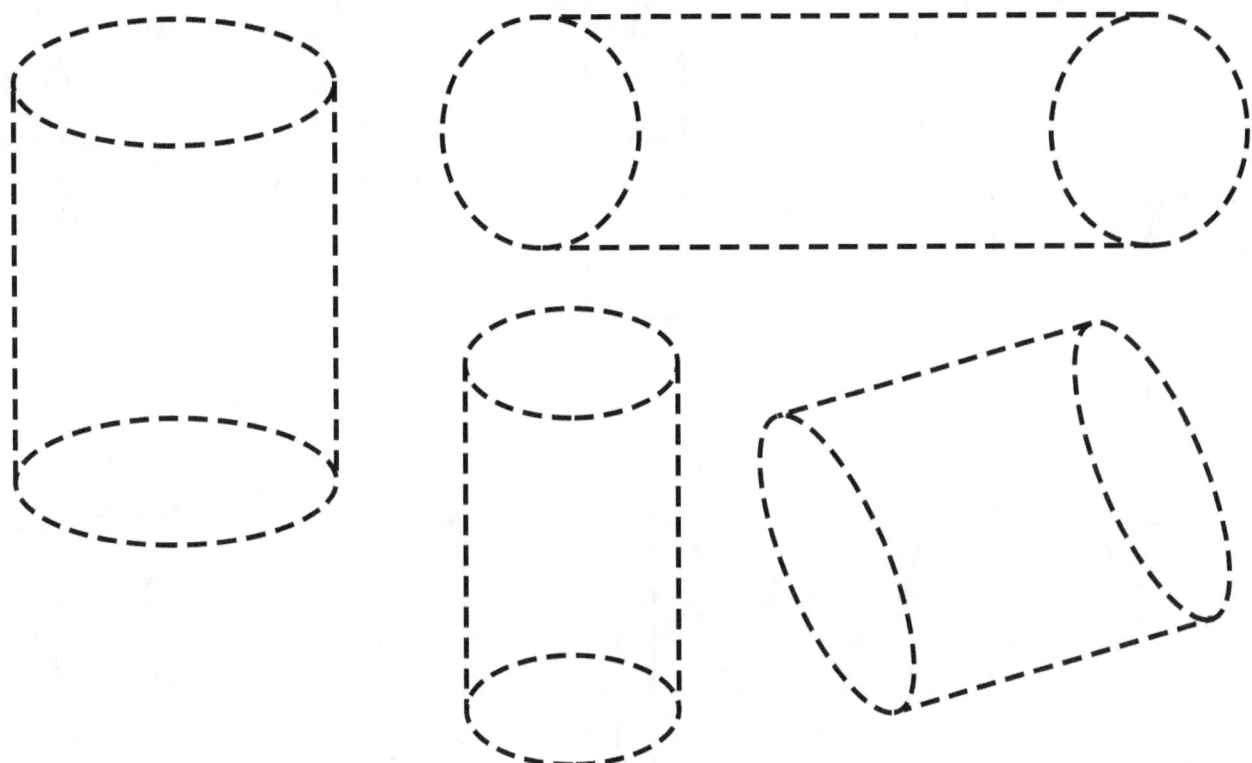

Trace the word.

cylinder

Cylinder

Name:_____

Trace the **cylinders**.

Cylinder

Trace each **cylinder** and color the picture.

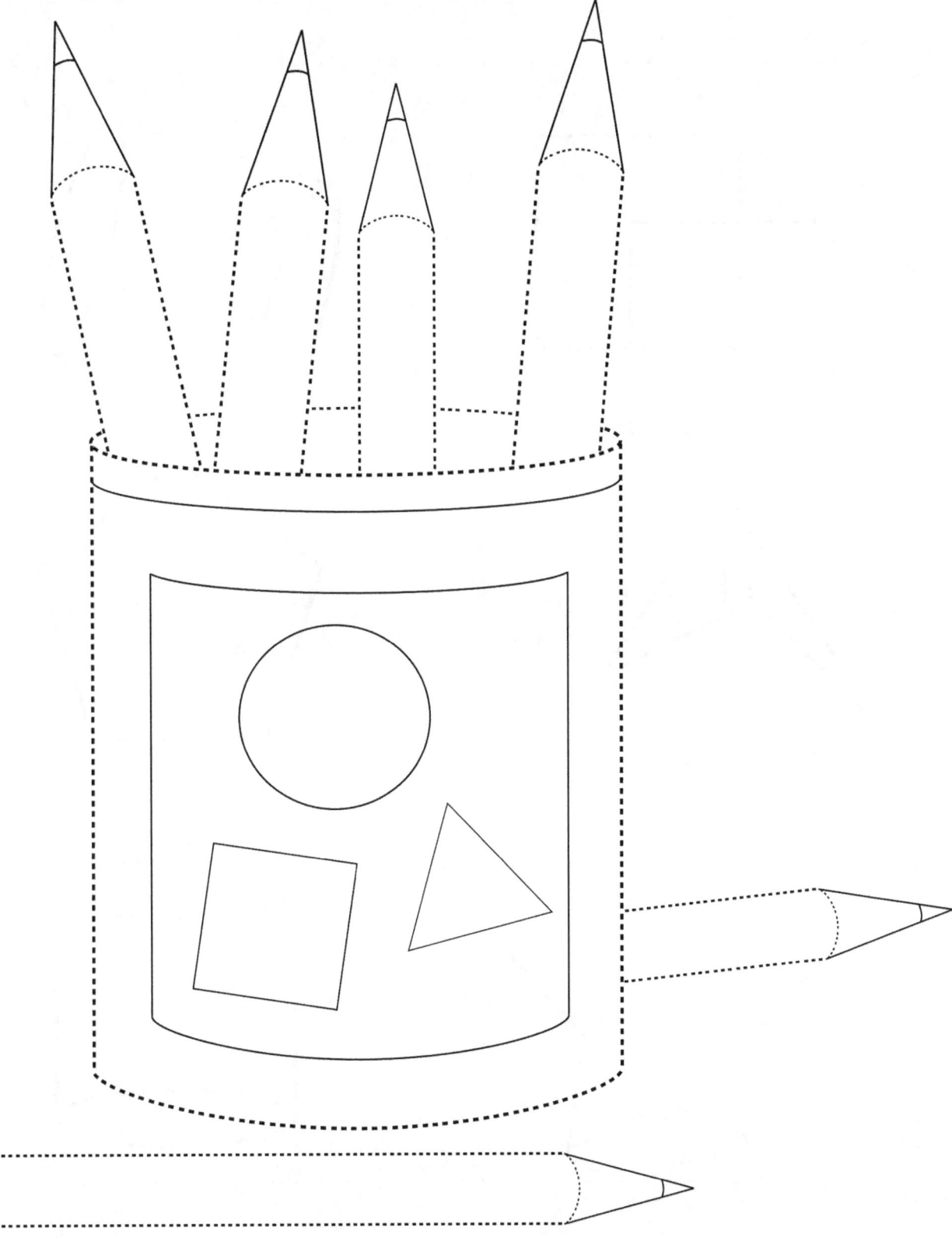

Cylinder

Color the **cylinder**.

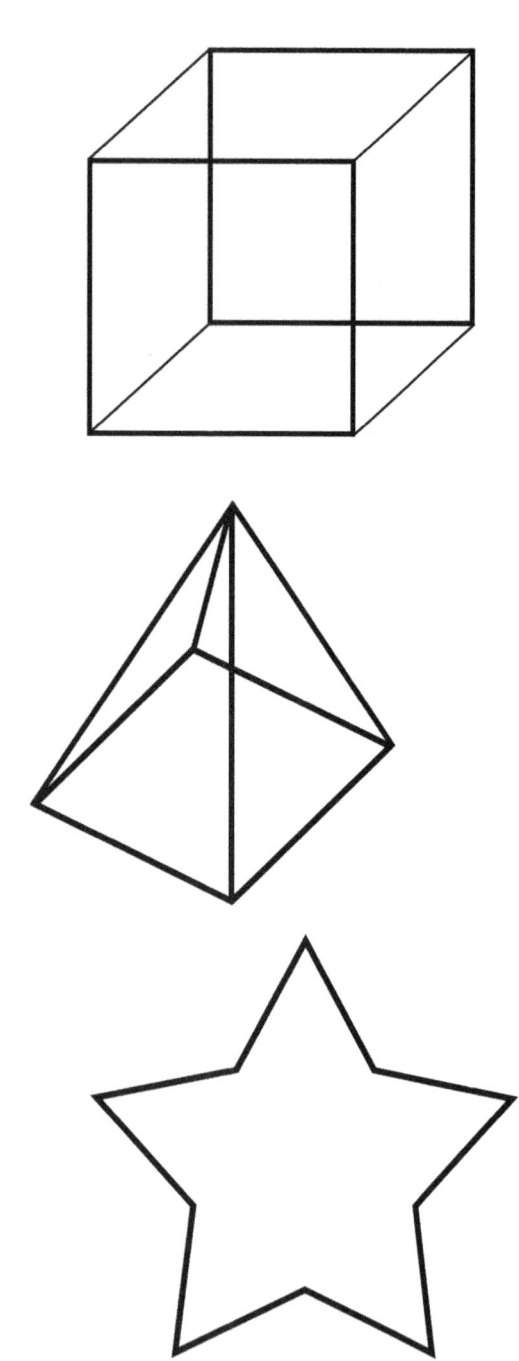
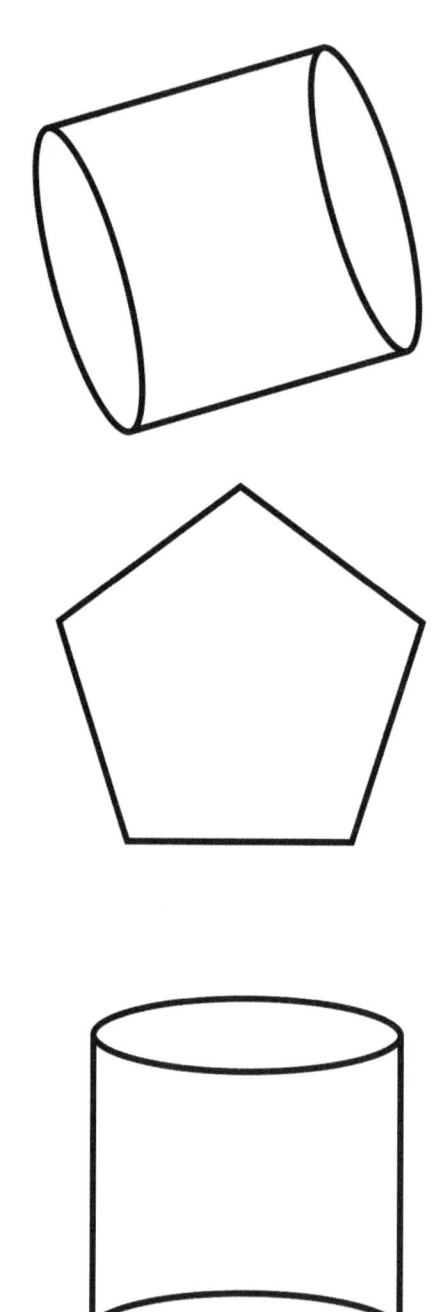

Name:_____

Trace, color and write

Trace and color each **cylinder** with the correct crayon.

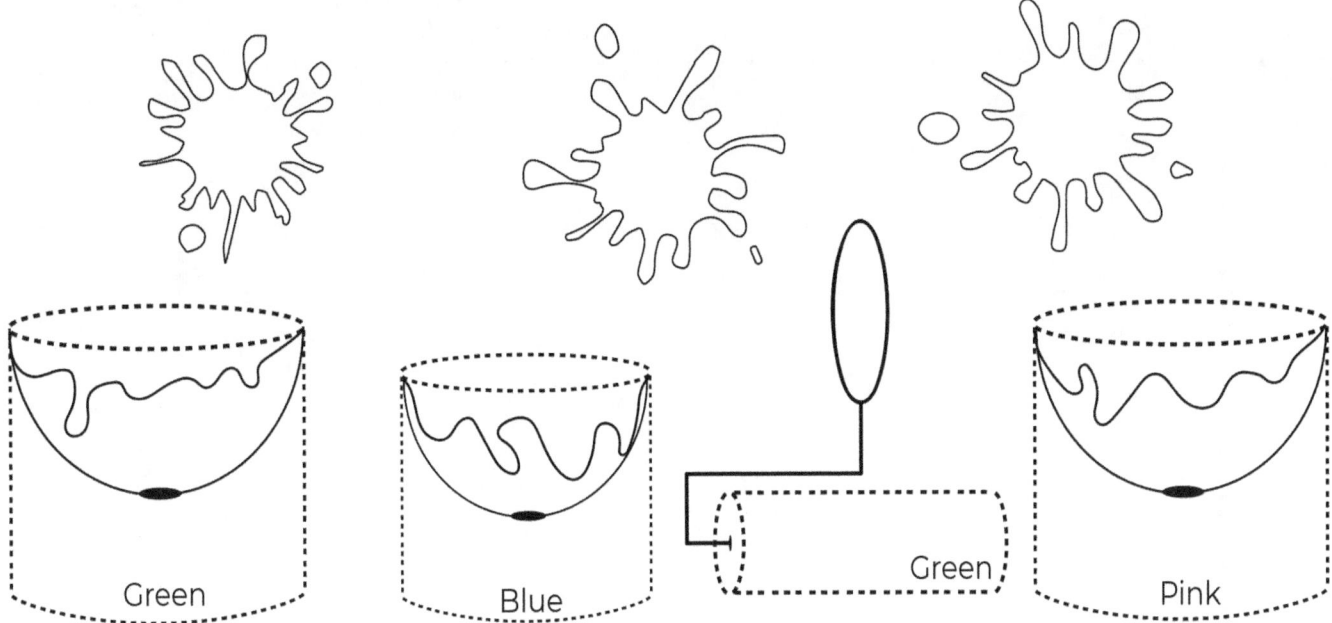

Read the word. Trace the word. Then, write the word on your own.

| cylinder | cylinder |

Name:_____

Cylinder

Practice drawing **cylinders**.

Practice writing **cylinder** *on your own.*

Name:_____

Shape review

*Draw a line to match each **shape** and color with the correct crayon.*

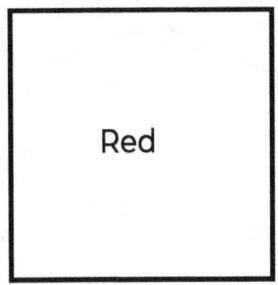
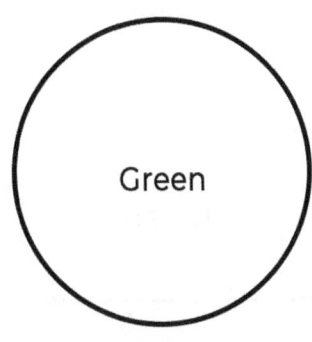
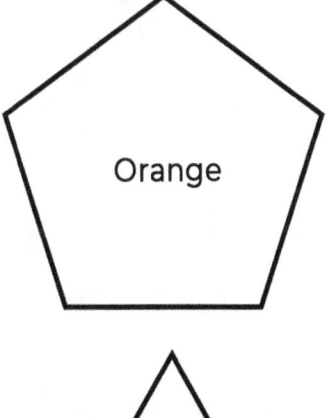
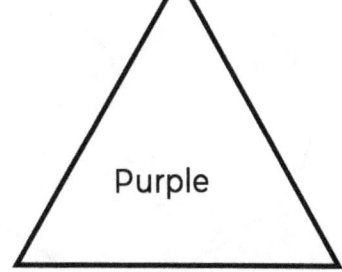
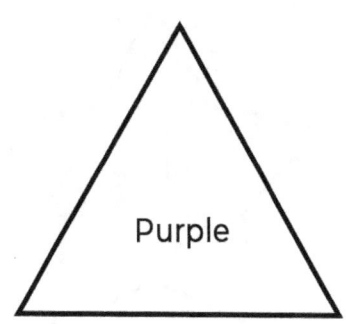

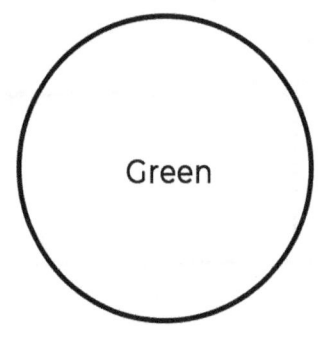
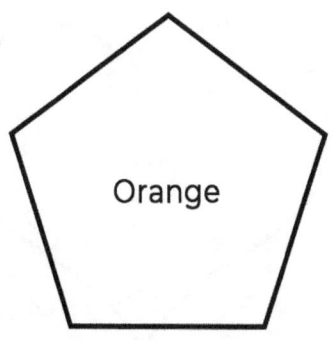

Name:_____

Shape review

Draw a line to match each **shape** and color with the correct crayon.

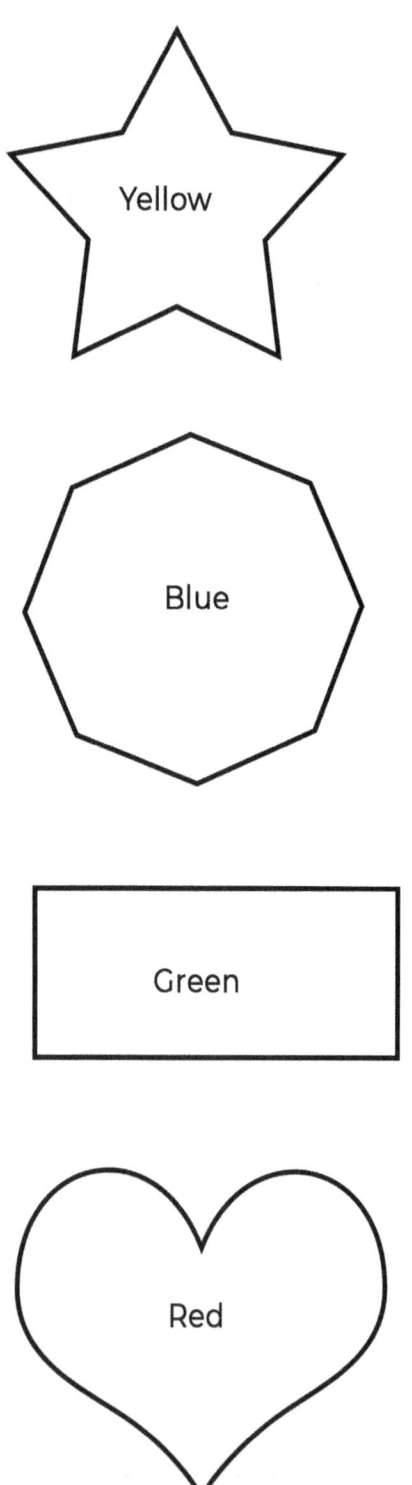
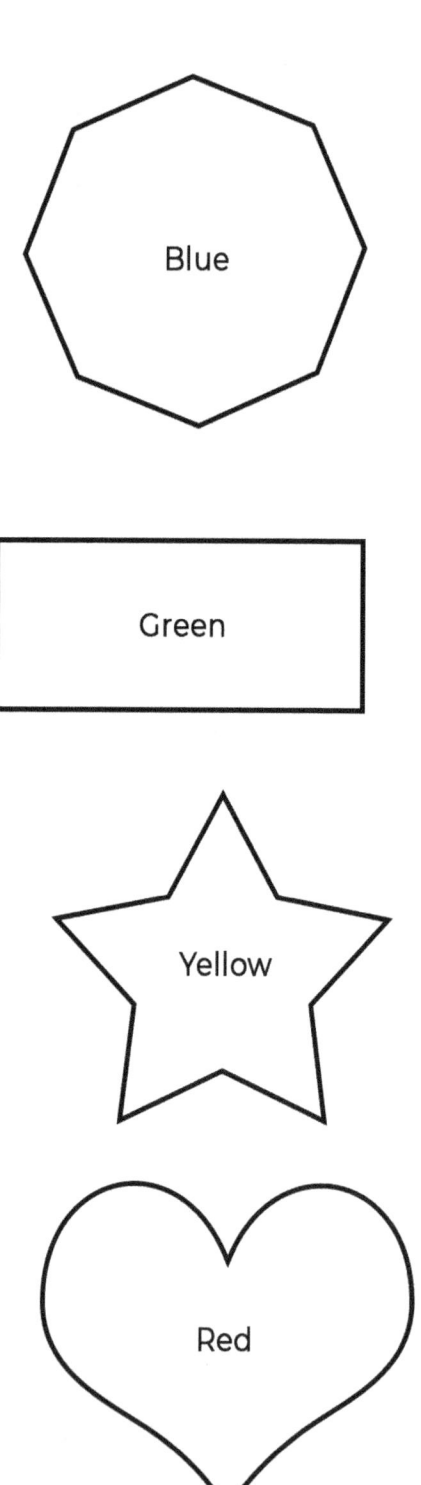

Name:_____

Shape review

Draw a line to match each **shape** and color with the correct crayon.

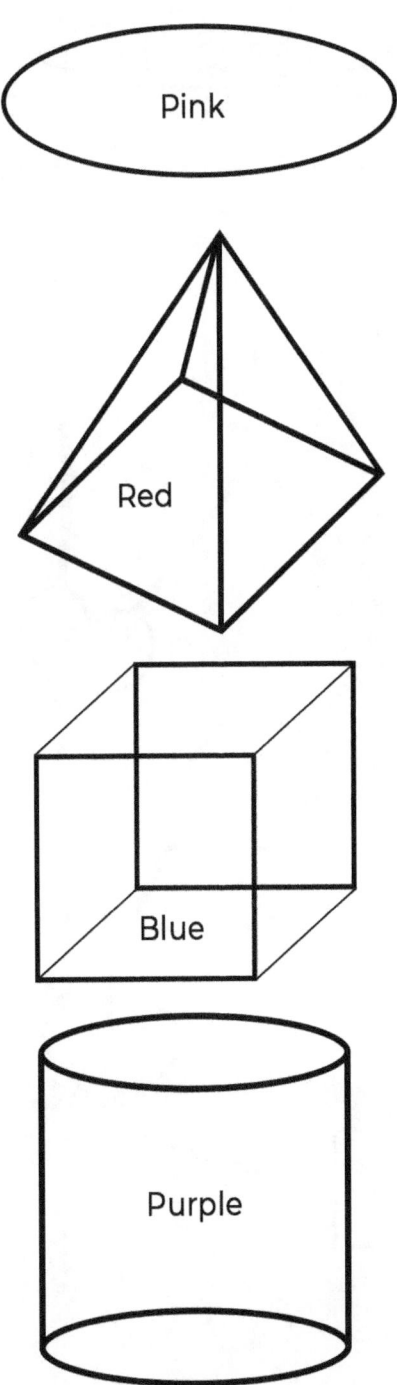
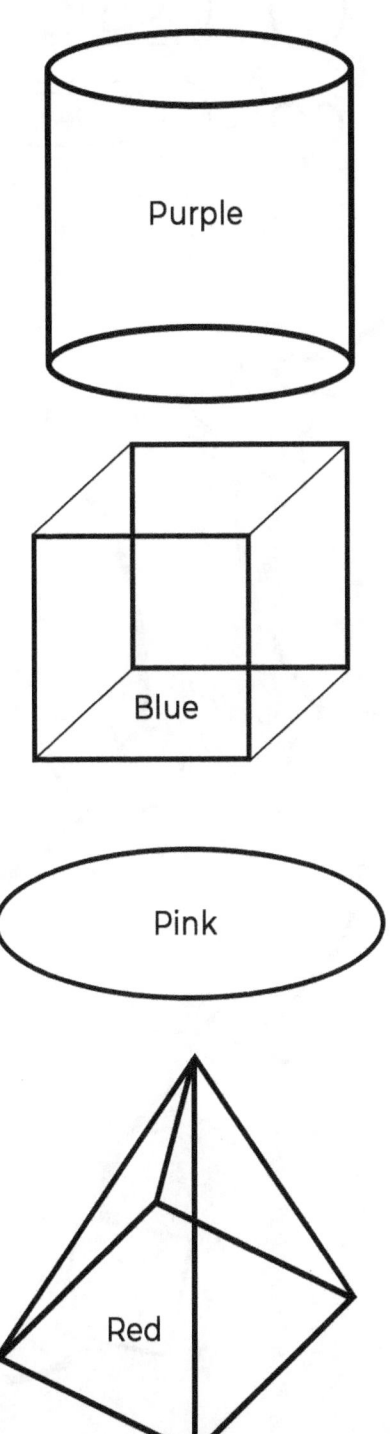

Name:_____

Shape review

Color each shape with the correct crayon.

◯ = (Green)   ☆ = (Yellow)

♡ = (Red)   ▢ = (Blue)

Name:_____

Shape review

Color each shape with the correct crayon.

▭ = (Orange)   △ = (Grey)

⯃ = (Purple)   ⬭ = (Pink)

Name:_____

Shape review

Color each shape with the correct crayon.

♡ = (Blue)   ⬢ = (Yellow)
☆ = (Pink)   △ = (Green)

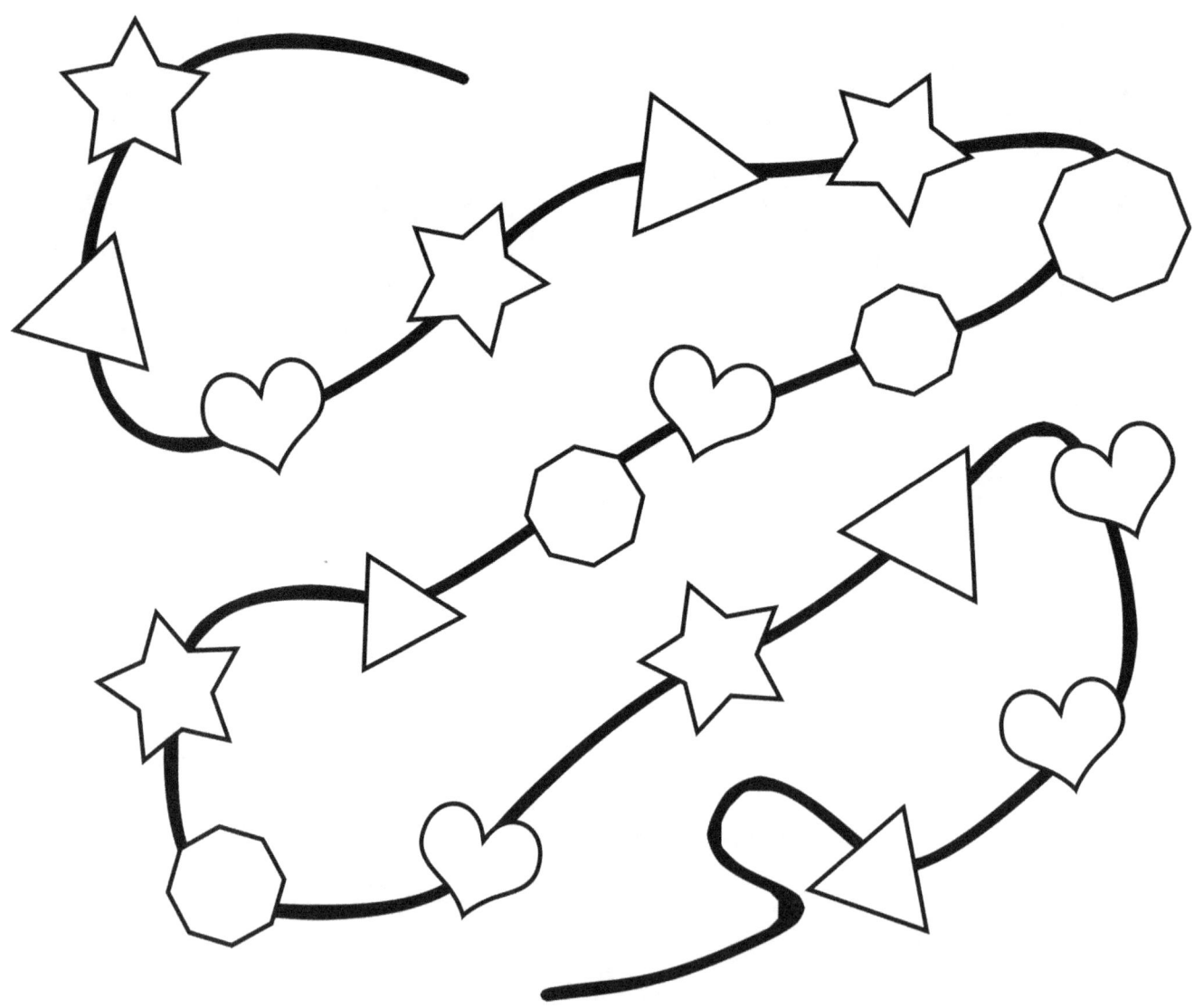

Denver International SchoolHouse   107

Name:_____

Shape review

Count and color each shape with the correct crayon.

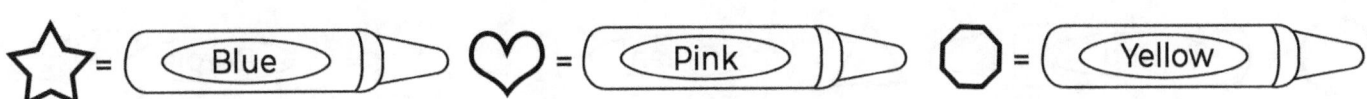

How many? ----------   How many? ♡ ----------

How many? ----------

Name:_____

Shape review

Count and color each shape with the correct crayon.

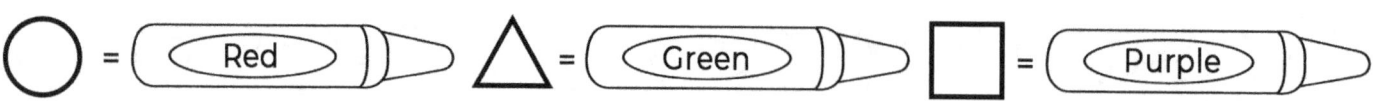

How many? ○ _____

How many? □ _____

How many? △ _____

Denver International SchoolHouse 109

Name:_____

Shape review

Count and color each shape with the correct crayon.

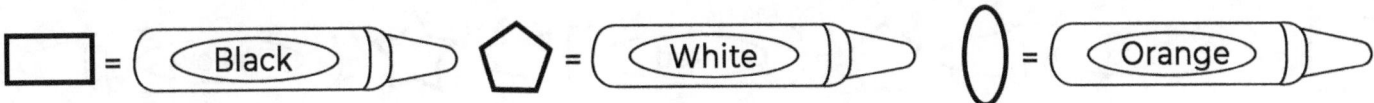

▭ = Black   ⬠ = White   ⬭ = Orange

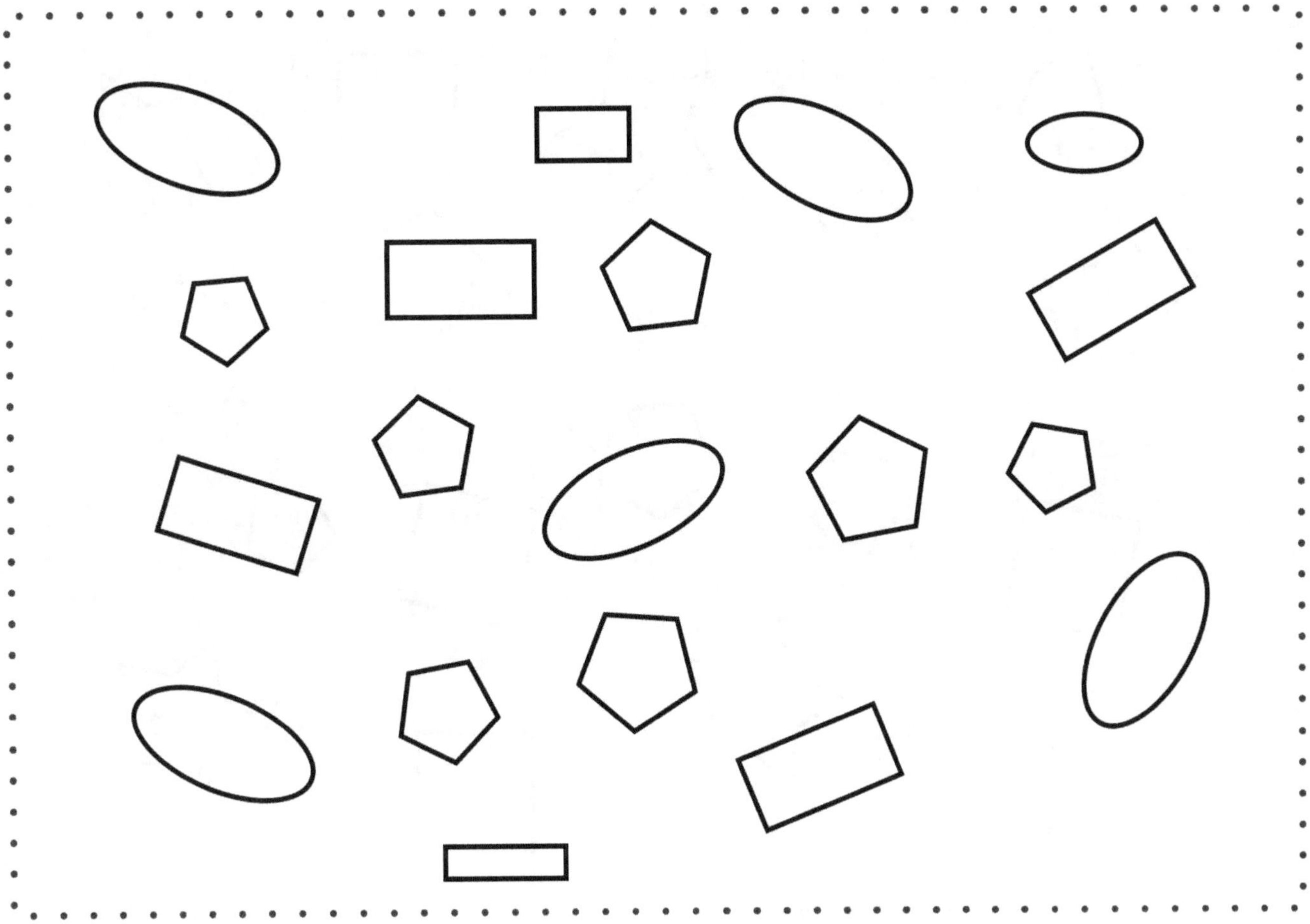

How many? ▭ _____

How many? ⬠ _____

How many? ⬭ _____

110   Denver International SchoolHouse

Name:_____

Shape review

Count and color each shape with the correct crayon.

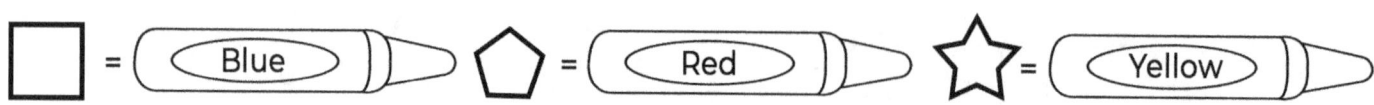

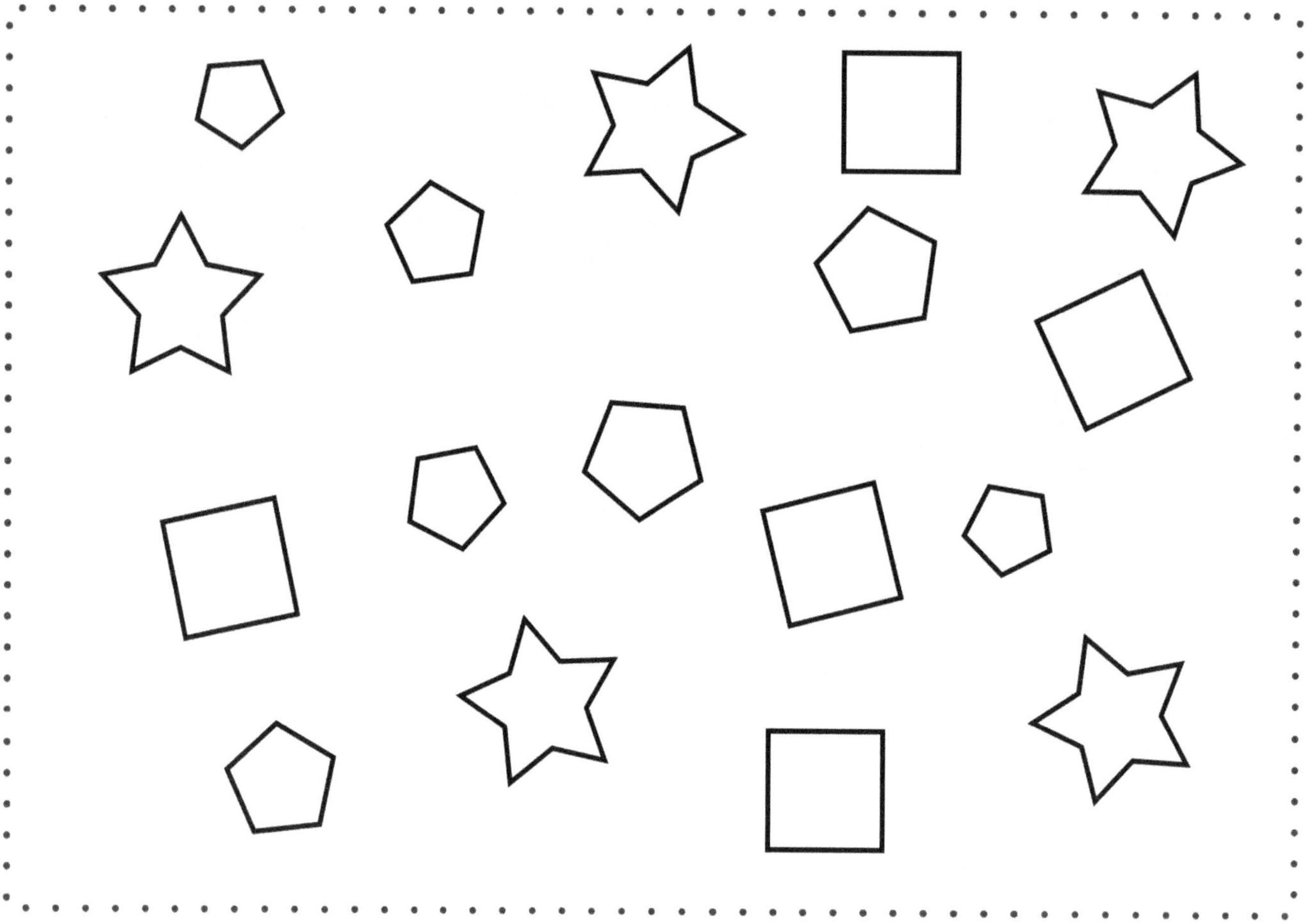

How many? ⬠ ----------

How many? ☆ ----------

How many? ☐ ----------

Denver International SchoolHouse   111

Name:_____

Shape review

Draw a line to match each shape on the left to an image with the same shape on the right.

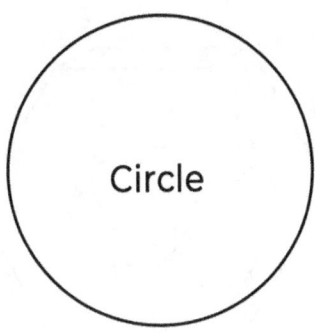
Circle

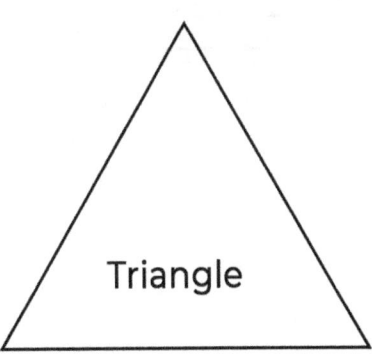
Square

Triangle

Trapezoid

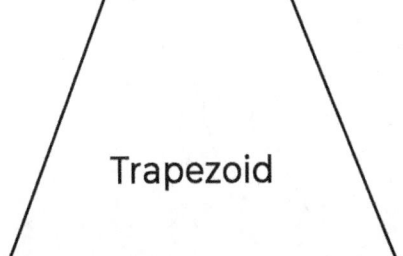

Denver International SchoolHouse

Shape review

Draw a line to match each shape on the left to an image with the same shape on the right.

Pentagon

Rectangle

Star

Hexagon

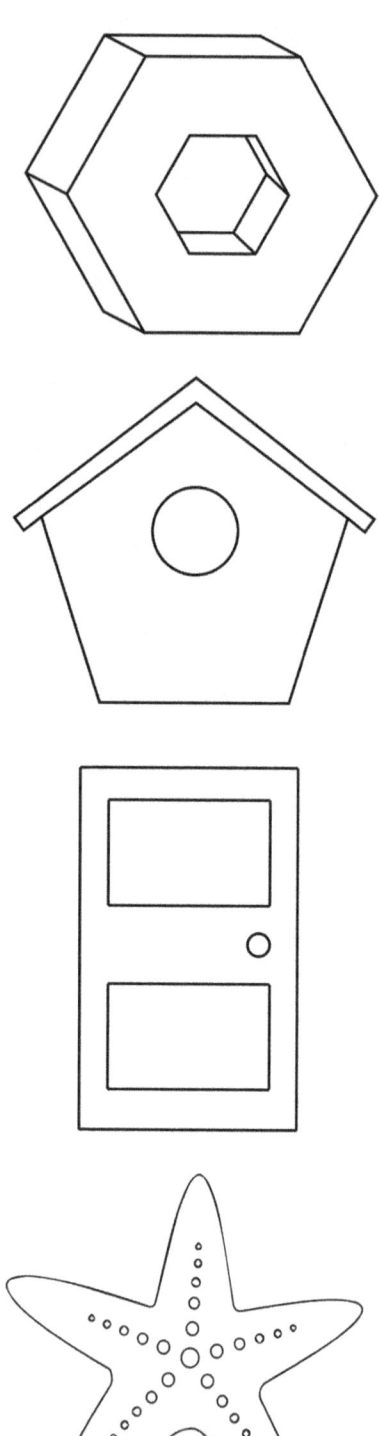

Name:_____

Shape review

Draw a line to match each shape on the left to an image with the same shape on the right.

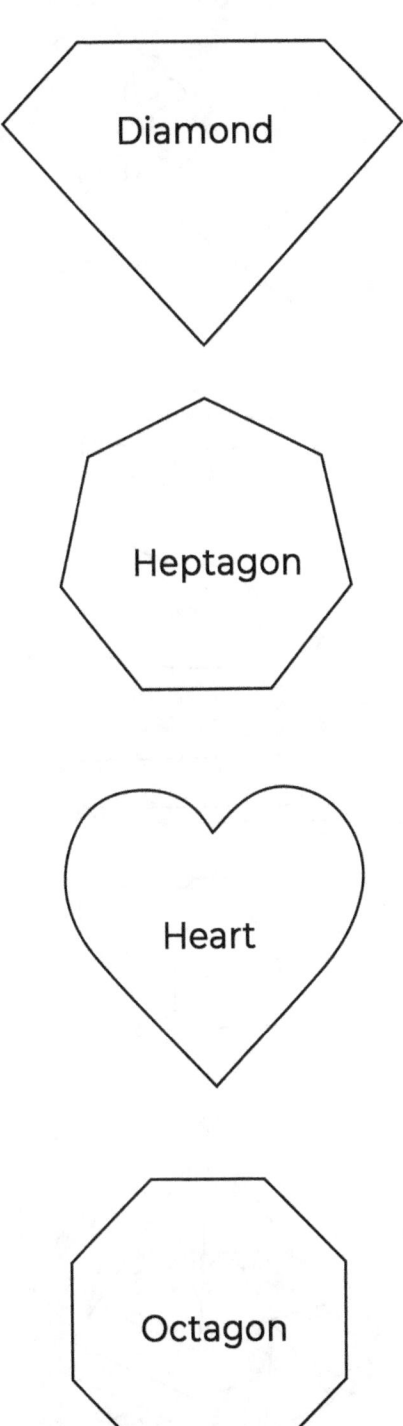
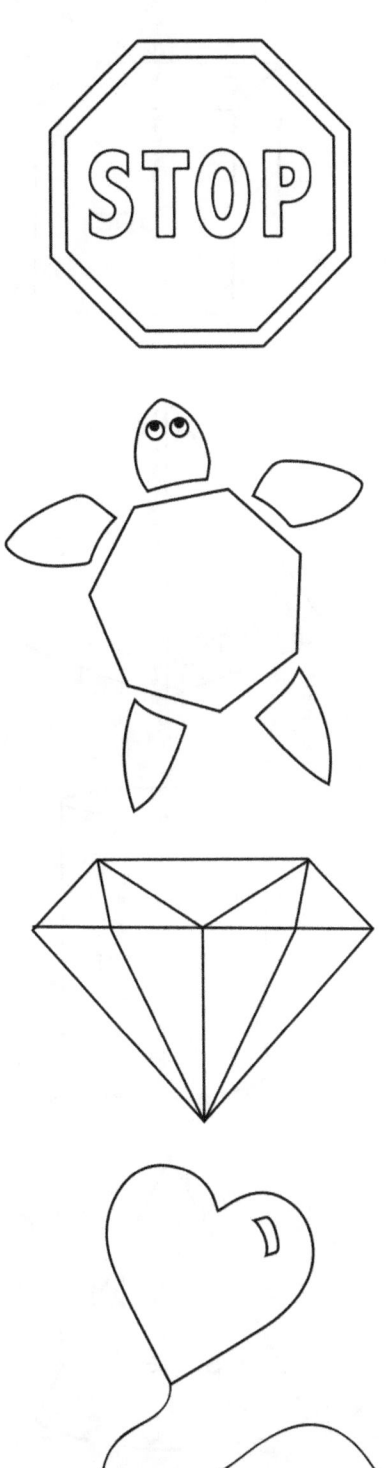

114 Denver International SchoolHouse

Shape review

Draw a line to match each shape on the left to an image with the same shape on the right.

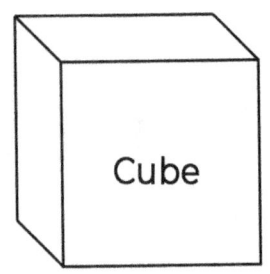
Cube

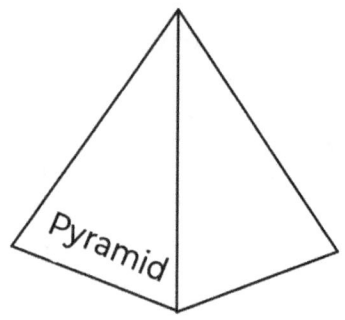
Pyramid

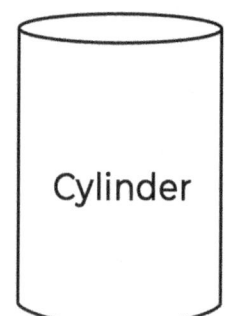
Cylinder

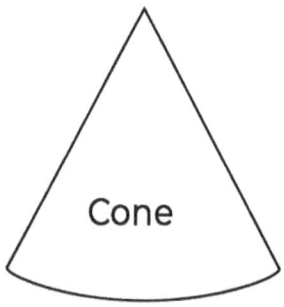
Cone

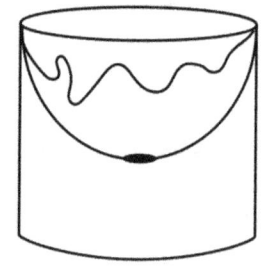

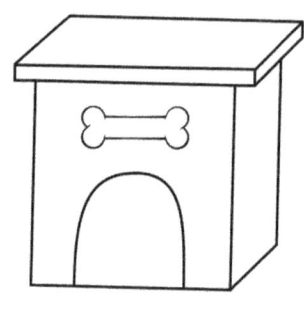

Shape review

Draw a line to match each shape on the left to an image with the same shape on the right.

Cylinder

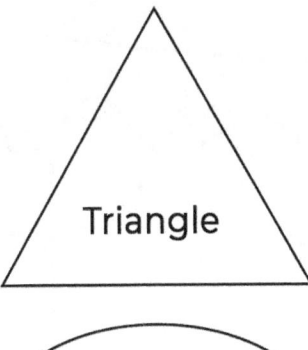
Rectangle

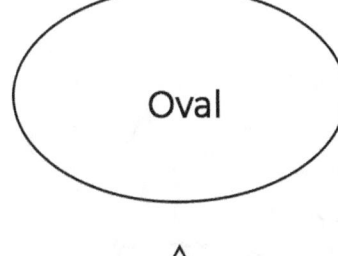
Triangle

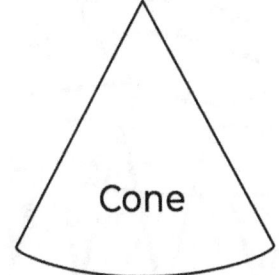
Oval

Cone

Denver International SchoolHouse

Name:_____

Shape review

Name:_____

Shape review

118 Denver International SchoolHouse

Name:_____

Shape review

Denver International SchoolHouse

Name:_____

Shape review

120   Denver International SchoolHouse

Name:_____

Shape review

Name:_____

Shape review

Name:_____

Shape review

Name:_____

Shape review

Name:_____

Shape review

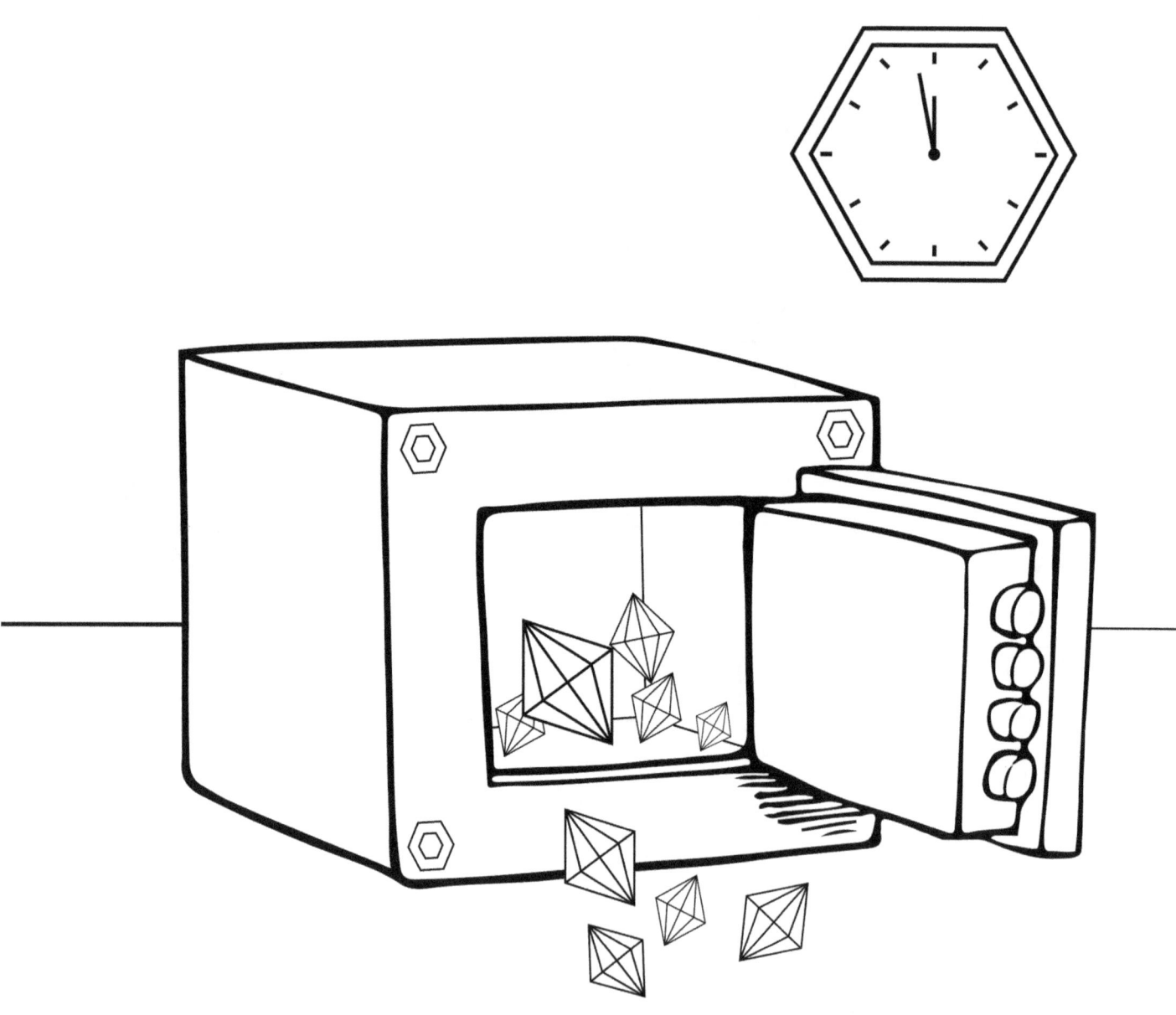

Denver International SchoolHouse

Name:_____

Shape review

Contact Us:

Web: www.dispreschool.com

Phone: (303) 928-7535

Facebook: @dispreschool

Twitter: @DISPreschool

Address: 6295 S Main St B113, Aurora, CO 80016